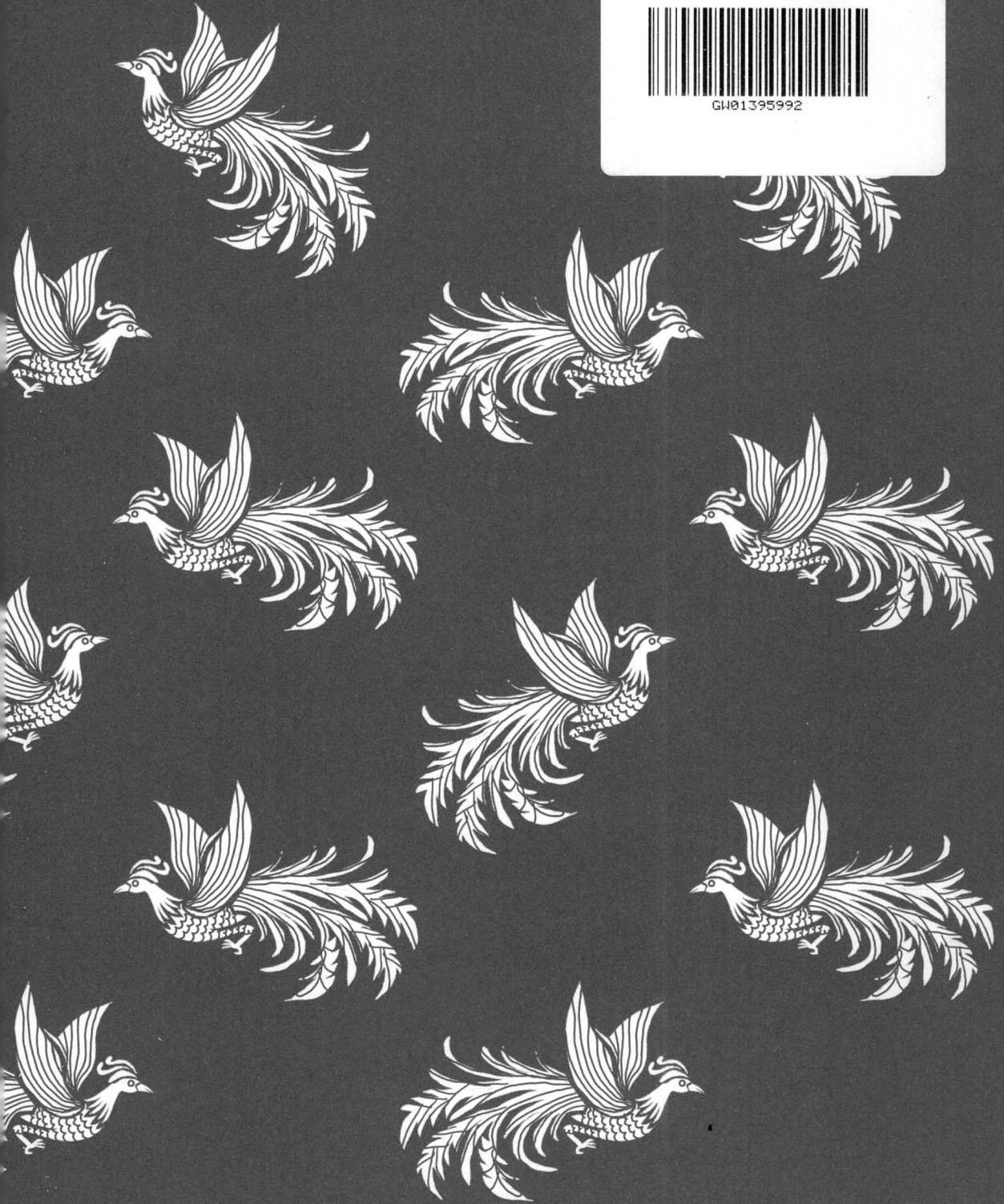

Chopsticks or Fork? is a love letter to the classics of the Australian Chinese restaurant. Lin Jie and Jennifer have written a book full of memories and nostalgia, but also full of hope for the future of this iconic part of our culinary landscape. I can almost taste the fried ice cream.

Adam Liaw

Chopsticks or Fork?, first the TV series and now the book, has completely and utterly won my heart. There is deep resonance here, not only for Chinese Australians, but also for anyone who has enjoyed a meal at their local Chinese restaurant. This is a point-of-view that I've longed to read, one that challenges the pervasive narrative of what Australian food is. I'm so grateful to Jennifer and Lin Jie for bringing us these stories of family and grit.

Hetty Lui McKinnon

A lovely insight into the world of Chinese food in regional Australia. Full of personal and touching stories, and well-written mouth-watering recipes, Jennifer and Lin Jie's book makes me want to travel around Australia to eat at these restaurants – and cook the dishes at home.

Tony Tan

CHOPSTICKS OR FORK?

To all the *Chopstick or Fork?* families.
Thank you for telling us your stories, and for feeding us so splendidly.

To Mum and Dad, for giving me the boldness and courage to tell stories.
For my children, whom I hope these stories will intrigue, delight,
and illuminate.

Lin Jie Kong

To Mum, Dad, and AJ,
who don't mind that I can't hold chopsticks properly.

Jennifer Wong

Jennifer Wong & Lin Jie Kong

CHOPSTICKS OR FORK?

Recipes and Stories from Australia's Regional Chinese Restaurants

Hardie Grant

BOOKS

CONTENTS

MENU

The key to Chinese food is balance, which is something to keep in mind whether you're choosing entrees or mains. Always go for variety: a variety of cooking styles (steamed, deep-fried, stir fried); a variety of proteins (seafood, chicken, duck, beef, lamb, pork) and vegetables; and a variety of flavours (sweet and sour, salt and pepper, satay). You may have noticed that we've only included one dessert in this book. For an alternative to deep-fried ice cream, you can't go wrong with a plate of lovingly cut seasonal fruit.

The dishes in this book are designed to share, so a banquet-style meal for four to six people might include two or three entrees, a few mains, a rice or noodle dish, followed by dessert. For a weeknight meal for four, you could easily choose three mains (two meat, one vegetable) to go with a pot of steamed rice. Of course you can also make just one dish and have it with steamed rice. If you want to enjoy a plate of lemon chicken all to yourself, who are we to argue?

ENTREES

Spring rolls
New Bo Wa...25

Dim sims
Oriental Palace...64

Sang choy bao
Happy's Chinese Restaurant 91

Sesame prawn toast
Dunsborough Chinese Restaurant..................156

Chicken and sweet corn soup
Gawler Palace...196

Pan-fried potstickers
T's Chinese Restaurant...........................211

MAINS

SEAFOOD

Salt and pepper squid
New Bo Wa...26

Steamed barramundi
Toy's Garden 48

Stuffed bean curd topped with seafood
Happy's Chinese Restaurant 95

Honey prawns
Raymond's at Malua Bay 108

Sweet and sour barramundi
Happy Garden 129

Braised king prawns with garlic sauce
Pagoda Chinese Restaurant 176

CHICKEN

Tamarind chicken wings
Happy Garden 126

Chicken and potatoes
Happy Garden 130

Lemon chicken
Gawler Palace..192

DUCK

Chef's duck
Oriental Palace.......................................68

Deep-fried duck with chilli plum sauce
Pagoda Chinese Restaurant 179

BEEF

Dragon steak
Toy's Garden 51

Crispy steak in plum sauce
Gawler Palace..195

Beef with black bean
T's Chinese Restaurant..........................215

LAMB

Sizzling Mongolian lamb
Raymond's at Malua Bay 111

PORK

Five spice salt chilli pork chops
Dunsborough Chinese Restaurant..................159

Sweet and sour pork
Pagoda Chinese Restaurant 174

COMBINATION

Seafood combination bird's nest
New Bo Wa...29

VEGETABLES

Water spinach with garlic and chilli
Happy's Chinese Restaurant 92

Bok choy and Chinese mushrooms
Happy Garden 133

Satay vegetables
Dunsborough Chinese Restaurant..................160

RICE & NOODLES

Combination chow mein
Toy's Garden 47

Char kway teow
Oriental Palace.......................................67

Combination fried rice
Raymond's at Malua Bay 112

Xinjiang hand-pulled noodles with lamb
T's Chinese Restaurant..........................212

DESSERTS

Deep-fried ice cream
New Bo Wa...30

INTRODUCTION

Why does almost every Australian town have a Chinese restaurant? It's the question that drove us, Lin Jie Kong (director/producer) and Jennifer Wong (writer/comedian/presenter), to make *Chopsticks or Fork?*, a six-part ABC series about Chinese restaurants in regional Australia.

Lin Jie: One night, in search of dinner towards the end of a long road trip, I found myself at the RSL club in Karuah, a sleepy bayside town just north of Port Stephens, New South Wales. I feared it would be another night of choosing between chicken parmy and fish and chips, but was surprised to find a well-reviewed Chinese restaurant in the club.

All the Australian Chinese staples were there: sweet and sour pork, Mongolian lamb, beef and black bean sauce. But what really caught my eye was the specials board: mapo tofu, Sichuan beef, a whole fish. These were dishes that wouldn't be out of place in a big-city Chinatown restaurant, but all the way out here? I ended up sticking with two favourites – special fried rice and Peking pork.

The first bite of Peking pork was a revelation: juicy, crispy, and perfectly covered in sweet sauce. It was just as good as my favourite from Golden Century in Sydney, a plate that would have cost at least double the price in Karuah. Meanwhile, the special fried rice was generously covered with layers of BBQ pork, chicken slices, and prawns. Rolling myself back to the hotel, as content as a fat Buddha statue, I rang my creative confidante Jennifer Wong: 'You won't believe where I've just had the BEST Chinese meal!'

It's a big statement, but I honestly hadn't had such a fresh and high-quality Chinese meal like that in a long time. We traded questions back and forth: 'Why were these people in Karuah? Where were they from? Why were they running a Chinese restaurant, and how were they serving up such delicious food? Did the locals actually order mapo tofu? Could we travel around country Australia and ask these questions?'

'The first bite of Peking pork was a revelation: juicy, crispy, and perfectly covered in sweet sauce.'

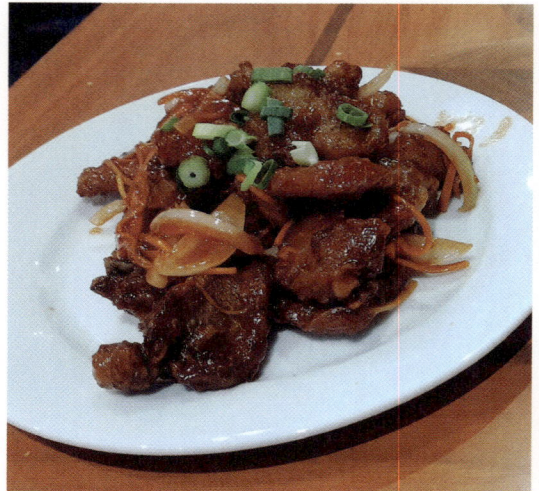

The pork that started it all!

Jennifer: In 2002, I was studying in Canberra and would sometimes go to Happy's Chinese Restaurant, which has been around since 1962. On a visit with my friend Tom Kwok (who, like me, is visibly Chinese), a waitress placed a pair of chopsticks on the table for me, and then asked Tom, 'Chopsticks or fork?'

We laughed about this for the rest of the meal: what was it about Tom that made the waitress offer him a choice? Was there something about him that suggested he'd find chopsticks a struggle?

Fast forward to 2020 and I'm at New Bo Wa in Moree with Lin Jie and our crew, Sue Lumsdon and Adam Toole, filming *Chopsticks or Fork?*. I watch in fascination as a table of eight eat spring rolls ... with knives and forks. I'd never seen anything like this before, but this was regular business for these diners, who'd been eating at the Bo Wa for forty years.

Travelling around regional Australia to interview families who run Chinese restaurants – and the diners who love them – has been rich with endearing revelations like this one. Right across the country, no matter where we went, we found stories about what it means to feel at home, whether you're the diner or the family running the restaurant.

Lin Jie Kong (left) and Jennifer Wong at Happy Garden in Darwin, NT.

The *Chopsticks or Fork?* crew with Gary Bong and family at Oriental Palace in Hervey Bay, QLD.

Lin Jie: There were many memorable moments while we were making this series. I keenly felt this moment of catharsis on our last shoot at Oriental Palace in Hervey Bay. The owner, Gary Bong, had invited friends and family for a huge 20th anniversary celebration dinner. I'm shooting all the way through and in the middle of Gary's thank you speech, I just start bawling and sobbing, and my camera is shaking. I look over and Jen's sobbing, too.

We couldn't stop crying. We were sniffling and blowing our noses afterwards, and Sue and Adam were like, 'What is wrong with you guys?' And it was just so hard to explain. Gary, like myself, had an immigrant childhood, and in that moment in the restaurant, seeing how proud his parents were of him, how proud his kids were, it felt like 'Wow, he's made it'. Like a lot of immigrant kids, you feel pressure to succeed. You want to make your parents proud, so that their move to a new country and culture is worth it. As a result, there's so much unspoken sacrifice, guilt and intergenerational trauma.

My parents ran a fish and chip shop for twenty years and in a way that experience was what propelled me to want to tell these stories. I think it could be said that no one starts running a Chinese restaurant in a country town because it's their life's ambition. Sure, a lot of people end up falling in love with the service, ritual, and community of the restaurant. But everyone starts in a position of necessity, usually one of economics. That night in Hervey Bay was a beautiful moment of seeing the community and Gary's family come together, beyond economic necessity. In my head, I hoped that my parents would also be proud of me when they watched this series.

Jennifer: When we were in Atherton, we filmed at the Hou Wang Temple. It's a Chinese temple, but also very Australian, in that the walls and roof are made with corrugated iron. Inside, near the elaborately carved altar, the local historian Gordon Grimwade pointed out two scuff marks on the timber floor. According to Gordon, the story was that a woman prayed there so often and so faithfully that she'd literally left her mark. There's no way to prove whether this is true or not. But that didn't stop Lin Jie and I from each placing a foot over those marks. We faced the altar and bowed at the same time, and for a moment there we were connected to countless Chinese people – former gold-diggers; fruit and vegetable farmers; maize growers – who had paid respects to the Hou Wang god in the 1900s.

The *Chopsticks or Fork?* crew with Vinh Chiem and family at Gawler Palace in Gawler, SA.

Sound recordist Adam Toole devouring another garlic prawn at Pagoda Chinese Restaurant in Atherton, QLD.

There are so many untold stories in Australia. To be able to tell a handful of stories about people you don't usually see on television has been a true honour. In total, we visited ten Chinese restaurants in regional Australia between 2020 and 2022, and spent time with the families who run them. We also invited people from around the country to share their Chinese restaurant memories, either as diners or as people whose families ran Chinese restaurants. Hundreds of people wrote to us, and we've included a selection in this book, with some memories dating as far back as the 1940s.

We hope *Chopsticks or Fork?* connects you to the people who create the familiar comfort and cosy deliciousness of your road trip meals, your memories of going to a restaurant for the first time, your Friday night dinners, and family celebrations over the years ... no matter your choice of eating utensils.

JENNIFER WONG & LIN JIE KONG

SALT AND PEPPER

NEW
BO WA

MOREE, NEW SOUTH WALES

For more than forty years, Moree locals have been heading to the New Bo Wa for prawn cutlets, sweet and sour pork, and deep-fried ice cream. It's also a regular spot for tourists after they've worked up an appetite soaking in the natural hot springs nearby.

Husband and wife, Ernest and Whitney Lai, have run the New Bo Wa since 2017. It was first opened in 1975 by Robert Wong from Hong Kong, and when he retired, he passed the restaurant over to Ernest's uncle-in-law, George. Although the restaurant has had three owners, the menu has hardly changed since the 1970s. And that's the way the locals like it. 'People go travelling to China and they order the sweet and sour pork. They come back and tell us they don't really like it,' says Whitney. 'They just like the Bo Wa's one.'

Ernest and Whitney moved to the agricultural town of Moree, seven hours north-west from Sydney, because they were sick of how rushed and crowded the big city was. 'We just wanted to change our lifestyle,' says Whitney. 'We were in Sydney, expecting our first baby, and we thought it's time to make a change.'

Ernest had gone to high school in Moree, but the first time Whitney came to Moree was when she moved there. She noticed that people in the country town of 13,000 were much friendlier than in the city. 'Here the people know each other and we say hello, and sometimes talk to them a little bit more,' she says. 'It's a very small community, but people actually support and help each other.'

Ernest found it pretty challenging when they first took over the restaurant. His day starts at 9 am and finishes at 9 or 10 pm, with a break between 2 pm and 4 pm. 'First of all, you have to run the whole restaurant, then you have to find the staff, which is hard because we are in a regional area,' he says. 'I also had to order the stock, which I hadn't done before, and manage all the stock, and I had to learn to cook from my uncle. Everything here is pretty much homemade: the spring rolls and the dim sims. And the vegetables we cut fresh, not frozen. We make our own sauces.'

The food was very different to what Ernest and Whitney ate at home, and much of it was new to Whitney, who's originally from Guangzhou (Canton) in China. 'We make lots of deep-fries here, but at home we don't deep-fry stuff frequently,' says Whitney. 'We usually just stir-fry or steam stuff, so it's a big difference. Sometimes I cook Western-style food, like spaghetti bolognese, because my kids love it.' Whitney's favourite dish in the restaurant is salt and pepper squid, and Ernest's favourite is the prawn cutlets. 'Probably because I make them,' jokes Whitney.

The last few years have not been easy for Moree; there was a devastating drought from 2017 to 2018. 'You can see, instead of the $200 takeaway, people might just have a couple of items for $50,' says Whitney. Just as the weather began improving and things started to look up, Covid hit. The restaurant shut for two months. 'We were lucky because we were still able to keep the doors open, and the customers could buy takeaway instead,' says Whitney.

For Whitney, one of the most rewarding things throughout this difficult time has been happy customers. 'This is the most important thing for me. Also, sometimes when you're working very hard and then you go home and you look at the kids and they smile...this is the most rewarding thing for me. Because it's long days and nights. To manage the restaurant and look after the kids as well, sometimes it's pretty tough.'

Their kids, Sophie, Kingsley, and Corey, are right at home at the restaurant, where Sophie folds red napkins into crowns, and Kingsley heads straight to the kitchen after school for a handful of cashews. Whitney and Ernest haven't put any pressure on them to take over the restaurant when they grow up, and so far it looks like the kids have dreams outside the restaurant. 'When I grow up, I want to be an astronomer or, I think I'm pretty good at giving advice. So, maybe a counsellor or a therapist,' says Sophie, the eldest. Meanwhile, Corey the youngest, wants to be a policeman, and Kingsley would like to be a gamer.

Country life has been good to the family, although the kids have occasionally experienced racism. 'Most of the time, because my parents own the Bo Wa, I get compliments at school for how good it is,' says Sophie. 'Sometimes, some racist comments, but I don't really mind. Although, they are rude.' Having lived in Moree for more than five years now, Ernest says that the moment he felt like he belonged to the community was when the kids started to have friends to play with. 'The kids feel like they're locals,' he says. 'They're not only Aussie kids, they're country Aussie kids.'

SPRING ROLLS

Spring rolls are a traditional snack in China, which are eaten to celebrate Lunar New Year (which is also known as the Spring Festival). That's why spring rolls are filled with fresh vegetables that traditionally would have only been available in springtime. The fact that they look like solid gold bars makes them a lucky food to eat for prosperity in the coming year.

MAKES 20

2 tablespoons vegetable oil

400 g beef mince

2 garlic cloves, crushed

2 cups shredded carrot

2 cups shredded cabbage

1 cup water

2 tablespoons salt

2 teaspoons white pepper

4 tablespoons cornflour

1 pack spring roll wrappers (20 sheets)

1 teaspoon cornflour, extra, mixed with 1 tablespoon water, for sealing spring rolls

4 cups vegetable or canola oil, approximately, extra, for deep-frying

Sweet and sour sauce (see page 129 to make your own, or use store-bought)

Heat the 2 tablespoons oil in a wok on high heat. Add the mince and garlic. Stir-fry until the mince is broken up and changes colour. Add the carrot, cabbage and water. Stir-fry until the vegetables have wilted. Add the salt and pepper and toss through.

Turn off the heat, drain the excess liquid from the wok and reserve. Add the cornflour to the reserved wok liquid and stir to dissolve. Set aside. Cool the mince mixture completely, then refrigerate for 1 hour.

To roll the spring rolls, lay a sheet of a wrapper with a corner facing you, add 2 spoonfuls of the filling 5 cm in from the corner. Fold the corner over the filling, then fold the left and right sides into the middle, then roll the wrapper up like a cigar. Seal using the cornflour mixture.

Heat the oil for deep-frying to 180°C in a small deep saucepan or wok on medium–high heat. Fry the spring rolls, in batches, turning occasionally, until golden. Drain on a plate lined with paper towel.

Serve with sweet and sour sauce.

SALT AND PEPPER SQUID

Cantonese-style salt and pepper squid is so well-loved in Australia that some have named it Australia's national dish. It's one of the most popular dishes at New Bo Wa (it also happens to be Whitney's favourite), and is an Australian Chinese staple for good reason. The lightly battered curls of squid are seasoned just-so, making them perfectly moreish. If you've never deep-fried anything before, it's worth learning how to deep-fry just so you can make this dish at home.

2 large squid hoods, cleaned

2 cups cornflour

vegetable or canola oil, for deep-frying

1 tablespoon vegetable oil, extra

4 garlic cloves, minced

1 bird's eye chilli, chopped

2 spring onions, white part only, chopped

½ teaspoon salt

½ teaspoon white pepper

¼ teaspoon chicken powder

BATTER

1 tablespoon plain flour

1 tablespoon self-raising flour

½ tablespoon cornflour

¼ cup water

Cut the squid into bite-size pieces and score a criss-cross pattern on the inside. Be careful not to cut all the way through the squid.

To make the batter, mix the ingredients for the batter in a large bowl. Add the squid and toss to coat the squid thoroughly.

Put the cornflour in a large bowl. Using tongs, coat each piece of squid, shake off excess and set aside.

Fill a large heavy-based saucepan approximately two-thirds full with oil. Slowly bring to 180°C over medium–high heat – this may take up to 10 minutes. Fry squid until crispy and golden then drain on a plate lined with paper towel.

Heat extra oil in a wok on medium–high heat, add the garlic, chilli and spring onion. Stir-fry until fragrant. Add the squid pieces and toss.

Serve squid sprinkled with salt, pepper and chicken powder.

SEAFOOD COMBINATION BIRD'S NEST

Bring a touch of the Cantonese banquet to your home with the seafood combination bird's nest (which you can actually fill with anything ... sweet and sour pork bird's nest, anyone?). This dish is traditionally served at special occasions, such as weddings and Lunar New Year, but there's no reason why you can't impress your dinner guests with it on a Friday night. At New Bo Wa, the stir-fry combination that Ernest serves is seasoned only by the chicken stock, so not as to overwhelm the delicate flavour of the seafood.

BIRD'S NEST

3 medium potatoes, peeled
1 teaspoon salt
2 tablespoons cornflour
vegetable or canola oil, for deep-frying
shredded iceberg lettuce, to serve

STIR-FRY

3 cups chicken stock
5 fresh tiger prawns, shelled, deveined with tails removed
5 scallops
5 pieces (80 g) squid, scored
5 slices (about 100 g) firm white fish of your choice
2 crab sticks, chopped
1 cup broccoli florets
½ cup sliced carrot
½ cup baby corn
3 button mushrooms, halved

CORNFLOUR SLURRY

2 teaspoons cornflour mixed with 2 tablespoons water

To make the bird's nest, slice the potatoes and cut into matchsticks. You can also use a mandolin with a julienne attachment or a julienne peeler. Rinse well under cold running water, drain and then pat dry with paper towel. In a large bowl, mix salt and cornflour. Add potato matchsticks and stir until well coated.

Arrange the potato mixture in a round metal strainer, and then put a second strainer on top to sandwich the potato and form a nest shape.

Fill a large heavy-based saucepan approximately two-thirds full with oil. Slowly bring to 130°C over medium–high heat. This might take up to 10 minutes. Fry the potato nest, still in the strainers, for about 3 minutes. Using tongs, gently remove the potato nest from the strainers. It should now hold its shape. Continue frying, turning occasionally until the nest is crispy and golden, around 2–3 minutes. Drain on a plate lined with paper towel.

To make the stir-fry, bring half the stock to the boil in a wok on high heat. Add the prawns, then after 30 seconds add the rest of the seafood. Cook, stirring, for another minute. Drain and set aside.

Heat the remaining stock in the wok until boiling, add all the vegetables and cook for 1½ minutes. Return the seafood, stir and cook for another minute. Add the cornflour slurry and stir until thickened. Remove wok from the heat.

Serve the potato nest on a bed of shredded iceberg lettuce, topped with the stir-fry.

DEEP-FRIED ICE CREAM

As desserts go, deep-fried ice cream is a joyful and thermodynamic wonder. To recreate this sweet childhood memory at home, remember: the oil temperature needs to be high (so in this case, a cooking thermometer would be especially useful), and speed is of the essence when removing the deep-fried ice cream from the oil and onto serving bowls. Make it once, and you'll most likely always have cake-coated ice cream balls at the ready in your freezer, just like a Chinese restaurant.

MAKES 4

500 ml vanilla ice cream

3 egg whites

3 cups breadcrumbs

4 slices madeira cake, ½ cm thick

vegetable or canola oil, for deep-frying

flavoured topping of your choice, for example: chocolate, caramel, strawberry

optional extras: wafer biscuit, whipped cream, maraschino cherry

Scoop out 4 balls of the ice cream, roughly 125 ml each, onto a tray lined with baking paper. Freeze for 1 hour.

In a bowl, beat the egg whites until slightly frothy. Place breadcrumbs in a separate bowl.

Remove the ice cream balls from the freezer, wrap each ball with one slice of the cake and smoosh together, forming a sphere roughly the shape of a tennis ball.

Working quickly, roll the ball in the breadcrumbs, press with your hands to firmly coat, then coat in the egg whites, followed by a second coat of breadcrumbs. Coat in egg whites and breadcrumbs once more.

Return the coated ice cream balls to the tray and freeze overnight.

When you're ready to serve them, fill a large wok or saucepan approximately two-thirds full with oil. Slowly bring to 200°C over medium–high heat. This might take up to 10 minutes.

Take the coated ice cream balls out of the freezer and, using a ladle, drop each one gently into the oil. Deep-fry until golden, about 20–30 seconds. Serve with your favourite topping.

THE HISTORY OF CHINESE PEOPLE AND CHINESE FOOD IN AUSTRALIA

Ever wondered why every country town in Australia has a Chinese restaurant? You might be surprised to know that the origin story can be traced all the way to the call of the goldfields in the 1800s, and possibly even further back. Chinese people have been eating Australian food – sea cucumber, specifically – since the 1700s, and Australian people have been eating Chinese food since the 1800s. It has, of course, changed a lot over time...

1700s: TRADING IN DELICACIES

In 2014, a Qing dynasty coin from China was found on Elcho Island off the coast of Arnhem Land, in the Northern Territory. The brass coin could have been minted as early as 1736 during Qianlong Emperor's reign. How such a coin came to rest on a beach in far remote Australia is actually due to a single food item: sea cucumber.

Long before European settlement in Australia, the Makassar people from the island of Sulawesi (now Indonesia) began visiting the top of the Northern Territory. From the early 1700s, they fished and traded with local Aboriginal people for sea cucumber, or trepang as they called it. They boiled down and dried their catch and later sold the prized culinary delight (and, some would say, aphrodisiac) to the Chinese in Singapore.

By the mid-nineteenth century, courtesy of the Makassar fleet, Australia was providing China with 900 tons of the in-demand invertebrate – around a third of their yearly consumption.

1800s: THE CALL OF THE GOLDFIELDS

In the 1840s, the first Chinese indentured labourers arrived in Australia, to cover the shortfall of labour, which arose when convicts were no longer shipped to the colony. These migrants ended up in kitchens and on farms around Australia, sowing the seeds of the gastronomic journey that was to come.

In February 1851, Edward Hargraves discovered payable gold near Bathurst in New South Wales and started the first gold rush. Lured by the sudden economic opportunity, Chinese migrants flocked to the country. By 1861, 3.3 per cent of the Australian population were born in China – a statistic that was not equalled again until the 1980s.

Cookshops and eateries sprung up in goldfields, towns, cities, and ports to feed the burgeoning Chinese population. They adapted their dishes and tastes to the local produce. For example, substituting Chinese greens with cabbage and using steak over pork or poultry. But not all of the clientele were Chinese. There's a famous sketch of John Alloo's Chinese Restaurant in Ballarat by Samuel T. Gill, where you can clearly see Caucasian faces tucking into roasts and plum puddings amongst the fried rice.

Once the gold dried up, many Chinese migrants returned to China, but new ones arrived to take their place (often the children of the first migrants) and they found other occupations, like market gardening, cabinet making, and laundering. This also caused a shift in the population towards cities and urban centres, creating thriving Chinatowns.

Not only were Chinese farmers nourishing the nation with fresh vegetables and fruit, Chinese chefs were delighting the white populace with twenty versions of sweet and sour sustenance.

1900s: EXCEPTIONS FOR CHINESE CHEFS

By 1890, around one-third of cooks in Australia were Chinese. But rising tensions, and in particular anti-Chinese sentiment, resulted in the White Australia Policy post-Federation in 1901. It's interesting to note that this was also the same year the government forbade Makassan boats from sailing to Arnhem Land, halting the by then two centuries old trade between both countries.

Due to the exclusionary immigration policy, by the late 1940s, the Chinese population in Australia had dwindled to 0.21 per cent. However, exceptions were made for chefs, so local Chinese businessmen established restaurants to bring workers and family members from China. These spanned the mum-and-dad staffed Chinese cafes with their laminated tabletops with dual Chinese and Western menus, to the upmarket, white table-clothed, folded napkin ventures, like Flower Drum in Melbourne.

By the 1960s and 1970s, hundreds of Chinese restaurants were established in Australian cities and country towns. Historian Sophie Couchman remarks 'Someone who leaves their home and immigrates to a new country is a risk taker. Once you've already travelled from China to Australia, moving across states is just the same. This is why you see so many Chinese restaurants in far flung country towns.'

2000s: CHANGING TASTES

Just as these older restaurants were shaped by early Chinese pioneers and immigration policy, so are today's new restaurants a product of their time. Around Australia, the classic old-school Chinese restaurant in many suburbs is making way for regional cuisine from mainland China, which reflects the vast array of immigrants who have arrived in the country in the last 40 years.

As the population changes, with 5.5 per cent of Australians having Chinese ancestry at the time of the 2021 census, people who go out for Chinese food in city centres these days are just as likely to tuck into Shanghainese soup dumplings, Sichuan hot pot, and Lanzhou beef noodles as they are to enjoy old favourites like sweet and sour pork, and beef and black bean. As tastes change, it's hard to predict what other regional Chinese cuisines will become popular in Australia. One thing we'll bet on though, is the enduring appeal of finishing a meal with the Australian Chinese classic that is a deep-fried ice cream. There really is no 'topping' that.

THE GREAT WALL OF HORSHAM

TOY'S GARDEN

HORSHAM, VICTORIA

Seventy-three-year-old Leon Toy, bottle of beer in hand, perches on a Ming dynasty-style porcelain stool in the foyer of his Chinese restaurant. Tonight, Toy's Garden Restaurant is closing for good, after Leon first opened it forty-eight-and-a-half years ago. His final dish as the restaurant's chef: a seafood omelette. 'I can't believe it's all over,' he says.

Leon left Hong Kong for Australia by himself at the age of twelve, in 1962. His grandfather, originally from Taishan in the south of China, arrived in the regional Victorian town of Warracknabeal in around 1914, and Leon's dad arrived in 1949. Because of the White Australia Policy, Leon and his mother were unable to join Leon's dad in Australia any earlier. The first time Leon met his Dad was when they were both in Hong Kong. By then, he was ten .

The Toys lived and worked in a market garden. After high school, Leon went to work at a Chinese restaurant in Brighton, in the south-east of Melbourne. 'I'm a creative person. In art theory in high school, we were taught that artists have to die before they are famous. I wanted to be an artist, but we lived in a market garden, so I had to run the business first,' says Leon.

In 1974, when Leon was twenty-three, an opportunity came up to open his own Chinese restaurant on the main street of Horsham. Before long, the restaurant was doing so well that they were turning away fifty diners every night. It wasn't all to Leon's liking, however. He was miffed that customers kept ordering chicken chow mein, a chicken and cabbage fried noodle dish. 'For ten years, I was cooking nothing but chicken chow mein. I said, "Chinese food is more than chicken chow mein." So I took it off the menu.'

In 1987, Leon moved to a larger restaurant in Horsham, which could seat 200 people. It was a full house the first night. By then, Leon was travelling overseas every few years to learn new dishes. From Mongolia, he brought back Mongolian beef, and from Hong Kong he brought back dragon steak. Eventually, he was even able to convince diners to eat whole steamed fish.

As well as changing the tastebuds of Horsham – a 'Tidy Town' known for wheat and wool – Leon changed its landscape by building a classical Chinese garden around the restaurant, complete with a mini golf course. It's all protected by a Great Wall of China made from fifty pallets of mason stone. For inspiration, Leon visited the UNESCO World Heritage-listed classical gardens of Suzhou in China, where some of the oldest gardens are around 2000 years old. It's a testament to his creativity and desire to be an artist, from the arrangement of Australian gemstones that dot the bridge he designed, to the rows of peonies that bloom as large as cauliflowers. 'I don't know how I did this,' Leon says under the willow tree he planted, 'But I did it.'

By Leon's side in the kitchen has been his wife May Har – who estimates that she's made one million spring rolls at the restaurant since she arrived from Hong Kong in 1976 – and his youngest daughter Melika, who's equally at home working the wok station as she is on the floor managing staff. Melika jokes that she's been working at the restaurant since she was six years old, setting the table and folding napkins since it relocated in 1987. 'I think I'm due for long service leave,' she says with a laugh.

With the restaurant finally closing, Melika knows that it's the staff and customers she'll miss most. Over the years, the restaurant has become the kind of place where everyone drops by for a coffee, even when it's not open. But there are some aspects that she won't miss so much. 'It's actually kind of hard educating customers how to eat Chinese food. You have a table of four and you have four people order lemon chicken. That's not what you do. You should order one lemon chicken, one steak dish, one fish, one rice. And everyone should share their food,' says Melika. They're lessons that many diners know, whether they're hungry tourists en route from Adelaide to Melbourne, or the five generations of locals who've eaten and often worked at Toy's Garden restaurant. Even the real estate agent who recently sold the restaurant drove deliveries for Leon as a teenager.

One local, Andrea Cross, came to pick up the last ever takeaway order at Toy's. Andrea worked at the restaurant when she was seventeen and has been dining at the restaurant for forty-one years – she and her husband have been there every Sunday night since they got married. 'Did we really appreciate them enough?' she wonders out loud as she waits to collect her Peking pork. 'Especially during Covid, when they were doing takeaway. They showed us all what it meant to keep going.'

When asked what she would do for Sunday dinner now without Toy's, Andrea stops to think. 'Maybe a Sunday roast?' Sundays are going to be different for Leon, too. Golf. Painting. Tending to his peonies, which he's taking with him from the garden. And, for dinner with May Har, perhaps a whole steamed fish.

COMBINATION CHOW MEIN

Leon learned how to make this classic Cantonese staple when he was an apprentice at a Chinese restaurant in Brighton in the 1960s. It's been on the menu at Toy's since the restaurant first opened in 1974. In a typical Hong Kong restaurant, it's the kind of dish that you might order for lunch at yum cha, or as part of a late-night feast. With a delicate combination of meat, seafood, and vegetables on a decadent bed of crispy fried noodles (ticking all the major food groups), it truly is a meal perfect for any time of day.

150 g chicken, diced into 2 cm cubes

1 teaspoon cornflour

salt and pepper, to season

350 g egg noodle, fresh or rehydrated

1 cup vegetable oil, to fry noodles

3 tablespoons vegetable oil, extra

½ brown onion, finely sliced

4 raw tiger prawns, shelled and deveined, tails intact

½ carrot, finely sliced

3 medium broccoli florets

3 medium cauliflower florets

1 cup roughly chopped bok choy

1 cup roughly chopped wombok

3 shiitake mushrooms, sliced in half

1½ cup chicken stock

150 g char siu (Chinese barbecued pork), finely sliced

1 tablespoon shaoxing rice wine

CORNFLOUR SLURRY

1 teaspoon cornflour mixed with 1 tablespoon water

In a small bowl, combine chicken with cornflour and a pinch of salt and pepper. Refrigerate for 20 minutes.

Sprinkle the noodles with salt. Heat the oil in a wok on medium–high heat. Add the noodles and fry until crispy, around 90 seconds. Press down on the noodles with the back of a ladle to shape into a flattish disc as it's frying.

Drain and discard the excess oil from the wok then flip the noodle disc and fry in the residual oil left in the wok until crispy on the other side. Remove noodles from wok and set aside on a serving plate.

Return the wok to medium–high heat. Add 2 tablespoons of extra oil and the onion, chicken and prawns and stir-fry until the chicken is cooked through and prawns have changed colour. Drain on a plate lined with paper towel and set aside.

Heat the remaining oil in the wok on high heat, add the vegetables, mushrooms and chicken stock and stir-fry until vegetables are tender. Return the cooked chicken and seafood and onions to the wok with the pork.

Add shaoxing wine and pepper, to season and stir-fry for 1 minute or until mixed well. Stir in cornflour slurry to thicken the mixture.

Serve noodles topped with combination mixture.

STEAMED BARRAMUNDI

Whole fish served with bones intact may be a challenge for diners in regional Australia, but Leon has made sure that the community in Horsham have absolutely embraced this dish. The barramundi is cooked Cantonese-style: lightly steamed, covered in fragrant herbs and bathed in a light soy sauce. The whole fish provides a stunning centrepiece for the table and its delicate flesh holds its own sweetness against the savouriness of the soy. It's a must-have for Lunar New Year, where serving fish with the head and tail intact symbolises wholeness, and a good start and end to the year.

1 small whole barramundi (around 1 kg)

1 ½ teaspoon salt

3 tablespoons light soy sauce

⅓ cup coriander leaves, roughly chopped

5 cm piece fresh ginger, peeled and cut into matchsticks

3 spring onions, cut into matchsticks

3 tablespoons vegetable oil

In a large saucepan, boil 1 litre of water and place your steamer on top.

Sprinkle fish with salt and place on a serving plate that can fit into the steamer. Steam for about 18–20 minutes until cooked.

Take the fish out of the steamer. Pour the soy sauce over the fish. Sprinkle with coriander, half the ginger and half of the spring onion.

Heat the oil in a saucepan or wok on high heat. Add the remaining ginger and spring onion. Stir a few times and then pour the oil mixture over the fish to serve.

Tip: This recipe also works well with frozen barramundi. Simply add an extra 10–12 minutes when steaming.

DRAGON STEAK

On a trip back to Hong Kong, Leon discovered this dish in the famous Mandarin Oriental Hotel. Luckily the hotel's master chef was kind enough to teach Leon how to make it. Dragon steak is reminiscent of sweet and sour pork but with a more complex flavour to go with its fiery name. Leon is super chuffed to share the top-secret recipe for this Horsham favourite, but perhaps not as chuffed as his customers, who have been asking him for this recipe for years.

350 g beef (skirt steak), sliced into thin strips
1 egg, lightly beaten
3 tablespoons cornflour
vegetable or canola oil, for deep-frying

MARINADE

½ teaspoon salt
½ teaspoon sugar
½ teaspoon white pepper
1 tablespoon soy sauce
1 tablespoon cornflour
2 tablespoons water

BATTER

¼ cup self-raising flour
150 ml water

SAUCE

2 tablespoons vegetable oil
1 small brown onion, finely sliced
1 small red capsicum, diced
2 tablespoons oyster sauce
2 tablespoons tomato sauce
2 tablespoons Sweet and sour sauce (see page 129 to make your own, or use store-bought)

In a large bowl, combine the beef with the ingredients for the marinade. Let sit for 20 minutes.

To make the batter, combine the flour and water in a small bowl. Adjust accordingly to achieve a thin pancake batter consistency.

Massage the egg into the beef mixture so the meat is coated evenly. Then add the cornflour and mix evenly. Pour the batter mixture over the beef mixture and mix to lightly coat the beef.

Fill a large wok or saucepan approximately two-thirds full with oil. Slowly bring to 180°C over medium–high heat. This might take up to 10 minutes. Gently lower in the beef, making sure to separate the strips. You may have to deep-fry the beef in batches depending on how large of a wok or saucepan you have.

Once beef is golden, drain on a plate lined with paper towel and set aside. You can fry the steak twice for extra crispness.

To make the sauce, heat 1 tablespoon of oil in the wok on a medium–high, toss in onion, capsicum, oyster sauce, tomato sauce and sweet and sour sauce. Stir-fry for around 1 minute.

Toss the beef in the sauce and coat well, remove from heat and serve.

PANTRY STAPLES

You're only ever a few simple ingredients away from cooking the recipes in this book. Most large supermarkets will have everything you need in the Asian aisle. For some of the sauces, you might need to go to an Asian grocer, where they'll have all the 're-sauces' you need for Chinese cooking.

LIGHT SOY SAUCE

Soy sauce is one of the most important ingredients in Chinese cooking, and has been used in China for more than 2000 years. It's made by fermenting soybeans, which results in soy sauces of different colours and potencies. Light soy sauce is saltier than dark soy sauce, and also has a thinner consistency and lighter colour. This soy sauce is used for cooking and also as a dipping sauce.

DARK SOY SAUCE

Dark soy sauce is fermented longer than light soy sauce, which makes it a darker colour and more viscous. It has a mature and deep flavour with caramel undertones, and is used to add colour to marinades and cooked dishes. Recipes will often use both light soy sauce (for flavour) and dark soy sauce (for colour).

SHAOXING WINE

This traditional rice wine from Shaoxing, a city in the Zhejiang province of China, is made from fermenting glutinous rice, water, and wheat. Some grades of rice wine are good enough to drink, but these days shaoxing wine is mostly used for cooking. It's a sweet and dry alcohol, which adds aroma and complexity to any dish, and is used in marinades, fillings, stir-fries, braises and sauces. A good substitute is dry sherry.

VEGETABLE OIL

Soybean oil and vegetable oil are traditionally used in Chinese cooking as they have a neutral flavour and can withstand the high temperatures of deep-frying and stir-frying in a wok.

TOASTED SESAME OIL

Chinese cooking uses toasted sesame oil very sparingly, usually for its flavour and fragrance. It's added in cold dishes, dipping sauces, and as the final aromatic touch in stir-fries, soups, and braises.

WHITE PEPPER

Used for its sharp, spicy and smoky flavour, the heat of white pepper is less intense than black pepper. It's often used in marinades for meat, poultry and seafood, and also sprinkled on soups before serving.

CORNFLOUR

Cornflour, also known as cornstarch, is the binding glue of Chinese cooking. It is used to marinate meat, create crispy coatings, and also in velveting meat to keep it moist and tender. Of course, no cornflour slurry would be complete without it, and this is used to thicken stir-fry sauces and soups. It's the ingredient that brings the silky texture and shine to so many Chinese dishes.

OYSTER SAUCE

This Cantonese sauce was traditionally made by boiling oysters and reducing the liquid into a dark brown sauce. These days, it's usually made with oyster extracts and seasonings. The thick, viscous sauce is salty, sweet, and full of umami, and is a versatile condiment that's widely used in Cantonese cooking.

HOISIN SAUCE

While hoisin sauce translates to 'seafood sauce' in Chinese, it actually doesn't contain any seafood. This thick, brown sauce made from fermented soybeans is sweet and fragrant, and is great for stir-fries and marinades (no barbecued pork would be complete without it), and can also be used as a dipping sauce.

PLUM SAUCE

Made with plums or other stone fruits, this thick, light brown sauce has a sweet and sour taste, and is perfect for dipping roast duck in. Plum sauce is also used for marinades and glazes.

BLACK BEAN SAUCE

This pungent sauce is made with salted fermented black beans, and is packed with flavour. You'll find it in the popular beef and black bean stir-fry, and also in steamed fish, and pork rib dishes, where a little goes a long way.

CHILLI BEAN PASTE

This sauce, known in Chinese as doubanjiang, is a staple of Sichuan cuisine. It's made with fermented broad beans and chillies, and has an earthy, salty, and fiery kick. It is often a key ingredient in spicy stir-fries and noodle dishes.

FORTUNE FAVOURS THE BAY

ORIENTAL PALACE

HERVEY BAY, QUEENSLAND

To celebrate Oriental Palace's twentieth year in Hervey Bay, owner Gary Bong ducks out of the kitchen to thank a restaurant full of friends and long-time customers for their many years of support. The people who've gathered tonight include some of the first friends he made in Australia when he arrived in 1992. 'Coming here from Malaysia with no friends and being the only Asian at Hervey Bay High, these two never ever treated me differently,' says Gary at the start of his speech.

By the time he goes to thank his family, almost everyone's eyes are wet with tears. 'I want to thank my beautiful children, Jeleen and Jovi,' Gary continues. 'Thank you for sacrificing. We don't get to see you, we never have dinner together except for Mondays. Our job, we have to work here six days a week. I hope you guys understand. I hope you guys know what we are doing it for.'

'Last but not least, my wife. Thank you, Aneliesa. I'm happy to wake up every day to see you. You're stuck with me forever. Thank you for giving up your job in accounting to be here with me. Hopefully I will give it back to you one day.'

Hervey Bay, a city of 56,000 people on Queensland's Fraser Coast, known as the whale watching capital of Australia, is a long way from Kuching, a small town in East Sarawak, Malaysia, where Gary and his family are from. The family sold everything to come to Australia in 1991. They brought with them $40,000, and when they arrived in Hervey Bay, Gary's dad, a mechanic, bought a second-hand car for $20,000. With the remaining $20,000, he went into partnership with another mechanic.

'And then Dad got cheated out of his money, and we lost everything,' says Gary. 'And I can see that it was really heartbreaking at that time. We had no money. We lived across the pier, and I had to go fishing and try to bring food to the table. I never complained about eating fish every day, even though I hated it. I just had to eat it, because Mum put the effort into cooking.'

Things continued like this for a few months until Gary's mum got a job, and the family began to eat meat again. Eventually, the Bong family took over Oriental Palace from Gary's uncle in 2000. Gary comes from a food family. In Kuching, which is well-known for its laksa, Gary's mum ran a laksa shop and his granddad ran a cafe.

Gary and his granddad often spoke on the phone about cooking. 'He always mentioned to me, "Make sure you don't use shortcuts" and "Do everything from scratch if you can",' says Gary. 'I said to Granddad, "Shortcut is always the best". You save time, you save labour. And he said, "No. In the end, you'll see the result, you are losing your customers".' Following his granddad's advice, Gary makes as many things as possible from scratch, like his popular dim sims, and a master stock that he uses instead of water.

The Oriental Palace menu proudly reflects the family's Malaysian heritage. The laksa is made Kuching-style, not with a curry base but with a sambal base, which is made using chilli peppers, shrimp paste, garlic, ginger, spring onions, palm sugar and lime juice. And unlike many laksas, the one at Oriental Palace doesn't have coconut milk. The sambal-based soup is flavoured with chicken bones and prawn shells, and comes topped with huge juicy prawns. 'We do have a lot of advantages because we have a lot of seafood from Hervey Bay,' says Aneliesa.

Char kway teow is another Malaysian dish on the menu that's become popular in recent years. Diners love these smoky flat rice noodles that are wok-tossed in pork lard and stir-fried with soy sauce, chilli, prawns, and bean sprouts.

Gary's not the only one in the family to share his love of food with the good people of Hervey Bay. After six years working in Brisbane, his younger brother, Elvin, felt the call of home and now has his own cafe, Vinvero, just a hundred metres up the road. 'Whenever I run out of anything, I just go and see him,' says Elvin.

The family has come a long way since arriving in Hervey Bay more than 30 years ago. 'Granddad would be very proud,' says Gary. 'We've come from nothing. It was very hard for us, but I never gave up. I always cook with my heart. I love my job.'

In April 2023, Gary and Aneliesa sold the restaurant and the family moved to Brisbane.

These days, Gary is studying nursing. Although he misses cooking for his customers and chatting with them, the decision to step away from a job he loved was driven by the duty he felt as a parent.

'When I was fourteen years old, my parents made the choice to come to Australia,' says Gary. 'Now my son is fourteen years old, it's time for me to make that choice to go to the city where there are more opportunities for my kids.'

Moving to Brisbane has also allowed Gary to make good on a promise. 'Aneliesa is working as an accountant now, just like I said that night in my speech, that I would make her dream come true.'

東興樓

ORIENTAL
PALACE

CHINESE RESTAURANT
• SINCE 1989 •

352 Esplanade,
Scarness,
Scarness Arcade

DIM SIMS

There's nothing better than a juicy homemade dim sim. Gary's version is a classic, no-fuss standard, yielding plump and tender morsels of deliciousness. The origins of dim sims can be traced back to yum cha, a Cantonese way of enjoying small eats (such as dumplings, and chickens' feet, and egg tarts) with tea. Many of the small eats are collectively known as dim sum (which translates literally as 'to point to the heart'). One of them is siu mai (or shumai), a pork-filled dumpling, which the Australian dim sim is based on. This recipe calls for steaming, but if you're feeling adventurous you can bust out the deep-fryer.

MAKES 16

400 g pork mince
½ cup chopped cabbage
½ cup rehydrated and chopped vermicelli noodles
2 tablespoons oyster sauce
1 tablespoon hoisin sauce
1 teaspoon salt
1 teaspoon sugar
½ teaspoon white pepper
1 teaspoon sesame oil
1 egg, lightly beaten
1 tablespoon cornflour
16 wonton wrappers
soy sauce, to serve

In a large metal bowl, combine mince, cabbage, noodles, sauces, salt, sugar, pepper, oil, egg and cornflour. Mix until well incorporated. Lift and throw the mixture against the bottom of the bowl 3 times to let the air out.

With one hand, make a 'C' shape in front of you, like you are holding a small cup. Place a wonton wrapper on top of the index finger and thumb. Add a heaped tablespoon of the filling in the centre of the wrapper and push it down into the space made with your fingers, while pinching the sides of the wrapper around the sides of the filling. Squeeze the top almost shut, then use the fork to fold the rest of the wrapper over the top of the dim sim. Repeat with remaining wrappers and filling.

Place the dim sims in a steamer basket, leaving space between them.

Steam the dim sims, in batches, over boiling water for 10 minutes. Serve with soy sauce.

CHAR KWAY TEOW

This rice noodle dish has a Hokkien name ('char' means stir-fried, and 'kway teow' means rice noodles), which suggests it might originally have come from Chaozhou in Guangdong. It became a popular dish in Malaysia and Singapore because of the large number of Chinese-born labourers there, who sold the dish as hawkers at night for extra income. Gary has simplified his famous char kway teow recipe from the restaurant for the home cook, to make it a one-wok dish: no par-cooking or transferring ingredients in and out of the wok. Just add in the ingredients step-by-step, keep stirring, and by the end you'll have a delicious dish. Make sure you get the wok up to temperature at the start to get that smoky wok hei ('the breath of the wok')

2 tablespoons pork lard or vegetable oil

1 egg, lightly beaten

1 garlic clove, minced

250 g wide flat rice noodles, fresh or rehydrated

¼ capsicum, sliced

¼ onion, sliced

100 g char siu (Chinese barbecued pork)

¼ teaspoon white pepper

1 teaspoon sesame oil

1 tablespoon oyster sauce

½ tablespoon kecap manis

½ tablespoon light soy sauce

½ tablespoon dark soy sauce

⅓ cup bean sprouts

2 spring onions, cut into batons, plus 1 extra, thinly sliced, to garnish, optional

Heat the lard or oil in a wok on high heat until almost smoking, add in the egg and the garlic, stir well until egg is scrambled.

Add the rice noodles and stir until noodles are loosened, then add the capsicum, onion and pork, stir-fry for 1 minute.

Add the pepper, sesame oil, oyster sauce and kecap manis. Stir-fry for 1 minute. Drizzle the soy sauces over the noodles and mix through.

Add the bean sprouts and spring onion, toss through until sprouts are slightly wilted. Remove from heat, add sliced spring onion to garnish, if using, and serve.

CHEF'S DUCK

Gary invented this dish as an homage to his grandmother's love of duck, and it has become the most popular item on the menu at Oriental Palace. He debones the duck for the restaurant as it makes it easier for customers to eat, but if removing the bones is too daunting, simply cut the duck in half and skip the deboning step. Serve it with bones intact.

1 whole duck, around 1.8 kg, cleaned and trimmed of neck, tail and excess fat (your local butcher might help you with this)

1 cup tapioca flour

1 cup rice flour

1 cup cornflour

2 cups vegetable or canola oil, for deep-frying

2 tablespoons hoisin sauce, plus extra to serve

MASTER STOCK

2 cups light soy sauce

1 cup dark soy sauce

1 litre water

2 cinnamon sticks

3 star anise

1 bay leaf

1 teaspoon fennel seeds

1 teaspoon cloves

50 g rock sugar

4 garlic cloves, smashed

3 cm piece fresh ginger, peeled and smashed

1 large spring onion, cut into batons

To make the master stock, combine soy sauces and water in a large stockpot or saucepan. Bring to the boil on medium heat, and then add all the other ingredients for the master stock. Reduce heat to simmer for 30 minutes with the lid on.

Add the duck into the master stock, breast side down. Bring to the boil, and then turn down the heat to low and simmer for 45 minutes with the lid on. Remove from heat and set aside to cool. Remove the duck from the master stock and drain well.

Crack the duck in half and gently debone each half. The duck meat should be tender enough for the bones to slide out.

In a large bowl, combine the flours and mix well. Coat the deboned duck halves in the flour mixture.

Fill a heavy-based saucepan approximately two-thirds full with oil. Slowly bring to 180°C over medium-high heat. This might take up to 10 minutes. Add duck, one half at a time, and fry each side until golden and crispy, around 1–2 minutes each side. Remove duck and drain on a plate lined with paper towel.

Spread 1 tablespoon of hoisin sauce onto the meaty side of each half. Turn skin side up and chop into 2 cm-wide pieces. Serve on a bed of steamed or stir-fried vegetables of your choice with extra hoisin sauce for dipping.

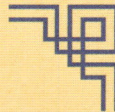

ONE MAN,
ONE MILLION KILOMETRES, AND 250 WONTON SOUPS

In the early 2000s, I travelled around Australia to take photos of Chinese restaurants. Behind the trip was what I call my addiction to wonton soup. At a rough estimate, I travelled more than one million kilometres, and visited more than 750 towns with one or more Chinese restaurants. I would say I ate at about 200–250 Chinese restaurants all up. The main dish I ordered was, of course, wonton soup. But for a change, I'd have hot and sour soup – largely misnamed because many weren't hot as in spicy and most were sweet rather than sour. The best one I had was a chilli soup in Longreach, Queensland.

To complement the photographs I took, I have a collection of more than 1200 Chinese recipes from historical newspapers and cookbooks. I did think about matching historical recipes with restaurants, but this would give the impression that the restaurants would actually have the dish on their menus. I doubt that any restaurant, let alone a Chinese restaurant, would have 'mahjong sandwiches' (1928) on their menu.

GRAEME LINDSAY

MEMORIES FROM AROUND AUSTRALIA

1940s–1960s

My dad, Bill Louey, was the first to open a Chinese restaurant in the south-west of Victoria in the 1960s: The Oriental Restaurant in Warrnambool. It was open late for when the pub closed, to cater to those who wanted a feed after a night out. My parents owned it for forty-eight years.

The Oriental, along with my uncle Kevin who owned another Chinese restaurant in town, introduced Chinese food to many Aussies. Warrnambool wouldn't have been the same without the Oriental Restaurant, The Dragon Inn and The Wok. Many of my friends also worked for my parents. Many students were taken in under the wings of my parents and the restaurant, and became our extended family.

We were the only Chinese family growing up in a regional town. And in those times racism was often dealt out. But being Australian-born Chinese, we were made to be resilient. We integrated well with others after often being made fun of. I was always quite ashamed and embarrassed by my heritage, as I just didn't want to be different.

JULIA MILLS

Our family restaurant was called the Yangtze Chinese Restaurant, in Cowra, New South Wales. It was one of the first Chinese restaurants to open here in the late 1950s. My dad, Bue Lo, better known as Bill, met and fell in love with my mother, Helen, and together built an amazing reputation for Chinese cuisine. There were many firsts for them: Mum being Australian and Dad being Chinese; they were the first interracial marriage in the community.

Dad's first restaurant was the Imperial Hotel in Cowra, where he found Mum after employing my nan as a kitchen hand. He saw a picture of Mum and fell in love with her then and there. As things developed, Dad and Mum set forth on their restaurant adventures. Dad taught Mum to cook the Chinese meals and in no time, people couldn't tell who cooked the meals. One funny memory I have is of Dad sitting at the till at the front door and people going to pay and telling him, 'Lovely meal tonight, Bill.' He would grin and say, 'Thank you', and it was dear Mum cooking away in the kitchen.

SUE JOHNSON

My Goong Goong (grandfather) ran the Yee Chong Restaurant in Chatswood, New South Wales from 1957 to 1982. It served fish and chips, and Chinese, and Australian meals. When making large amounts of food for the shop or a gathering, many hands made light work. Most dishes were made from scratch (no frozen spring roll wrappers in those days) and had multiple cooking stages. We were enlisted at an early age to help with cleaning fish, making dim sims, rolling spring rolls, peeling prawns, marinating beef, stuffing mushrooms, slicing, dicing, chopping, steaming, frying... We learned much more than just how to cook and eat food. While our hands were busy, we were subtly taught lessons of life, the value and rewards of work, patience, organisation, and more. There were long hours of preparation and trading, with only Sunday mornings off work. I used to think it was a 'holiday' to go to school.

JANICE LEONG

I was reared in Grafton, New South Wales, in the 1940s and 1950s, and one of the most exciting things was the opening of a small 'exotic' Chinese takeaway (with some Formica tables for dining in). It was in a little alley, behind one of the fruit shops, not really in the main drag of town. Of course, there was no plastic for takeaway so I was given the order for chow mein from Mum and I rode my bike with a billy can over the handlebars, to fill it with this exciting food. Home I raced, safely always as I remember. I can still taste the gloriousness of that chicken chow mein. The first of many, many Chinese meals over the years.

JAN BROWN

In 1950 when I was fifteen, I was taken to Dixon Street in Sydney to a restaurant called the Lean Sun Low. Its caption was 'famous for short soup', and there was a menu of approximately eight pages in which the first four pages were devoted to short soup. You name it, and it was there as short soup. The restaurant was far from what restaurants look like these days. The clientele were mainly labourers from the nearby wharves, and workers from the city's fruit and vegetable market, which was down the end of Dixon Street. To go to the toilet, you would walk through the kitchen past a row of ducks hanging up to dry.

One of my first meals after one of the short soups was curried prawns and chicken chow mein.

I have been enjoying Chinese cuisine for 72 years now and still enjoy it as much as ever.

I was recently at a Chinese restaurant and asked by a young Chinese waitress how long I had been using chopsticks. When I replied, 'About 70 years,' she was quite perplexed.

BILL MACKS

Growing up as a restaurant kid was not easy, especially in the 1960s and the 1970s at the Sun On Restaurant in Miranda, New South Wales. We were the only Asian family in the area and we lived above the restaurant.

My parents, Elaine and Peter Pingon, worked hard, and working at night was not conducive to family life. Being the eldest and the only girl, I took on the role of surrogate mother to my brothers. While my parents worked the restaurant at night, I looked after my younger brothers. I tried to make our lives as normal as possible and valued doing well at school. I took the attitude that we could be just like the 'Aussie' children, but we could be even better. We all excelled at school, perhaps seeing how hard our parents worked motivated us to achieve.

After school, Mum always had afternoon tea ready. We definitely had a gourmet feast, whether it be macaroni, chicken, sausage rolls or fried rice. Friends who may have come with us were certainly amazed at our gourmet spread. Our dinner would be made during the evening dinner service. Mum would prepare our meal and bring it up to us in between cooking meals for her customers. We ate really well. When Mum was in residential care, we talked about our life growing up in the restaurant and at the forefront of my mother's mind was to be able to feed her children. Later I understood that was Mum's way to express her love to us children.

DEIDRE AFTANAS

The Pagoda was a successful Chinese restaurant, which my parents owned during the 1960s and 1970s for almost twenty years after migrating from China with minimal English. We attended the local primary school down the road, and we would return to the restaurant for lunch every school day. All our friends were envious, but we would much rather have not been so different and wished we could have sandwiches and more time in the playground.

Together with my sisters I was able to help our parents from a very young age, not just in translation but also with the many jobs. We did everything from picking buckets of beans, packing fried noodles, folding serviettes, making spring rolls and fried rice, restocking the cans of drinks and cigarettes, and serving customers. The most challenging job was adding up the docket in the days before calculators!

My parents opened the restaurant every day of the year and worked from 9 am to 11 pm. We even opened on Christmas Day. We did eventually start closing the shop for a day each year on Chinese New Year. This was a special day as it was the only day that I can recall ever eating out with the family while growing up. The New Year was celebrated with a visit to the local Pizza Hut in Miami, as there was no such thing as a good Chinese restaurant to dine at then.

My parents still love to eat pizza and so Sunday's very Chinese dish of congee must be accompanied with a purchased family size supreme pizza.

RUBY LEE

IN THE MOOD FOR CANTONESE

HAPPY'S CHINESE RESTAURANT

CANBERRA, AUSTRALIAN CAPITAL TERRITORY

It's lunchtime at Happy's. While an Anita Mui pop song plays, a couple of tables of tradies are tucking into honey chicken, and sweet and sour pork with fried rice and cans of Coke. A mural of The Great Wall of China – painted by one of the owner's sons in 1975 – extends across the length of the underground restaurant, creating a dramatic backdrop for a Thursday lunch with the soundtrack of 1980s Hong Kong. Time slows down here.

Happy's opened in 1962. Once you head down two narrow flights of stairs in Civic, Canberra's central shopping area, you're oblivious to the fact that this much-loved institution – the first Chinese restaurant in Canberra (although this is its second location) – is now surrounded by Chinese food options ranging from Shanghai-style soup dumplings to biang biang noodles from Shaanxi.

It couldn't be more different to the Canberra that Happy Chan arrived at in the late 1950s, via Sydney and Queensland. He'd come from a village in Zhongshan, Guangdong (also known as Canton) as a vegetable farmer, but he hated mosquitoes and early starts, so he stopped farming and began working other jobs. He saved enough money and decided to open a Chinese restaurant in the Australian capital after first opening one in Queanbeyan in New South Wales.

'Things were really tough, in the sense that he was the only Asian guy in Canberra,' says Happy's grandson Gavin, who's now the third generation to run the restaurant. There was also the challenge of what to cook with. 'In 1962, there were hardly any fresh ingredients, and there were no Asian ingredients. It was all Australian vegetables, like broccoli and carrots, so the menu had things like T-bone steak and chicken with vegetables.'

Australian Chinese food was really different back then, says Gavin, and so were locals' attitudes toward this new-at-the-time cuisine. 'You could get a table of four, for example, and two of the people might not know anything about Chinese food, so they'd order off the Australian menu.'

One local remembers seeing on the menu a dish of T-bone steak with spaghetti, and sweet and sour sauce.

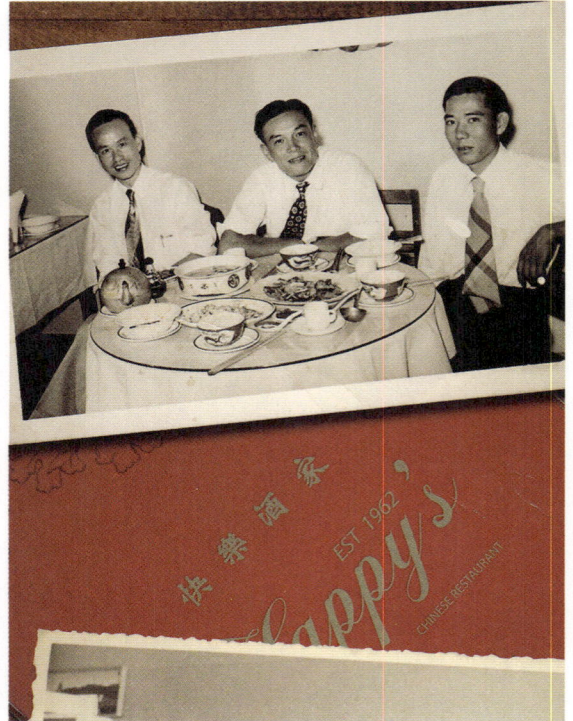

These days, diners come to Happy's for Cantonese cuisine, as much as they do for Australian Chinese classics like lemon chicken or sizzling Mongolian lamb. Chef's specials include stuffed bean curd topped with tofu, water spinach with garlic and chilli, and the humbly named pork stew, which Chinese readers can tell actually refers to the classic Hakka dish of braised pork belly with preserved mustard greens. The base for all their meals is a 16-hour master stock, which Gavin says is the biggest point of difference in their cooking – that, and the heat of the woks.

So how did Happy's transition from favouring the Western palate to offering more Cantonese-style food? 'When my grandfather retired in 1982, my uncle and my dad took over, and they did a little renovation of the place,' says Gavin. 'And that's when they sort of thought, okay, look, I think it's time now to change the food we serve. People are a little bit more accepting now, and there's more Asians, so maybe we can attract some new clientele.'

HAPPY'S RESTAURANT
CHINESE MEALS
快樂酒家
TAKE AWAY OPEN 7 DAYS
HAPPY'S CHINESE RESTAURANT
快樂酒家
CANTONESE CUISINE
OPENING HOURS
HIPPO CO
HIPPOCO.COM.AU
NOW OPEN

The 1980s was also a time when a lot of fresh ingredients started to make their way to Canberra, like tofu and Chinese broccoli, with more Asian immigrants and more Asian restaurants opening. Even though the food that was offered in the 1960s wasn't as splendid as it is now, the restaurant served an important purpose for many Chinese men.

'A lot of people got their foot in the door with restaurants at our restaurant,' says Gavin. 'They'd stay at my grandfather's place in Curtin, he'd teach them how to cook, and eventually they'd open their own restaurants in places like Lyneham and Cowra.'

The profession is one that Gavin didn't enter straight after school, although he's always been a part of the restaurant. 'I started serving customers and taking orders when I was about seven. I used to bring the plates in and stand on a box of canned corn so I could wash the dishes.'

He left Canberra when he was 17 and worked various jobs in Sydney for ten years, including managing a Coles supermarket, before returning to Canberra with his wife May to run Happy's in 2007. Because of staff shortages during Covid, their two oldest daughters, Emily and Rachel, have started helping out at Happy's. The youngest, Jennifer, can sometimes be spotted playing video games in a nook behind the cash register.

Today, Gavin's mum, Linda, still works in the kitchen, doing the frying and prepping. 'Mum is a first-generation workaholic. She just can't sit still. Even now, she's 67. We have Tuesdays off, and her sister's got a restaurant, and she'll go and work at her sister's restaurant to help out.'

Celebrating more than 60 years of a family business has been humbling for Gavin. 'There are customers now that I've known since school, since I was my little Jennifer's age,' he says. 'There's a table that comes down every Wednesday, basically, and has been coming for the last thirty, forty years. And they pretty much sit in that corner over there and have their lunch on a Wednesday. It's amazing.'

Meanwhile, for the tradies who've been lunching, their break is over. It's time for a final swig of Coke before returning to natural light. An energetic pop song by Sam Hui, the father of Cantopop, plays as they head upstairs – the sounds of 1976 accompany them back to the present day.

SANG CHOY BAO

Sang choy bao is a classic starter on every Australian Chinese restaurant menu. In Cantonese, the name means lettuce (sang choy) wrap (bao). The crisp, cold crunch of the lettuce yields to the piping hot meaty filling, plus there's the novelty of edible bowls! If you're making your own for the first time, here's a hot (or cool) tip from Gavin: after you cut the lettuce cups, put them in a container and cover with water, then pop them in the fridge until it's time to use them. It freshens up the lettuce and makes it that little bit crispier. Then when it's time to serve, give them a good shake to remove the excess water.

MAKES 4

2 tablespoons vegetable oil

200 g chicken mince

½ onion, diced

½ carrot, diced

2 shiitake mushrooms, diced

small handful finely sliced spring onion

1 garlic clove, minced

1 teaspoon fresh minced ginger

1 tablespoon oyster sauce

1 tablespoon soy sauce

1 tablespoon shaoxing rice wine

4 large iceberg lettuce leaves

Heat half the oil in a wok on high heat, add the mince and stir-fry until it changes colour and then remove and set aside.

Heat the remaining oil in the wok on high heat. Add all the vegetables, except the lettuce, and oyster sauce. Give everything a quick stir.

Add the mince back in, toss it through and cook for 1 minute. Stir in the soy sauce and shaoxing wine just before serving.

Spoon the filling into each lettuce cup, give them a good shake to remove any excess water and serve immediately.

WATER SPINACH WITH GARLIC AND CHILLI

This homestyle Cantonese dish of water spinach (also known as kang kong, ong choy, or morning glory) is an absolute crowd favourite at Happy's. The preserved bean curd gives it an extra funky kick. Gavin says it's crucial to get the wok nice and hot, and to toss the spinach through quickly to avoid overcooking, so it retains a bit of crunch and freshness. Choose the youngest, most tender bunches of water spinach you can find, to avoid stalks that are too chewy.

2 cubes preserved white bean curd with ½ tablespoon liquid from the jar

1 teaspoon sugar

2 tablespoons vegetable oil

1 cup chicken or vegetable stock

2 bunches water spinach, washed and cut roughly into 3 sections

3 garlic cloves, finely chopped

2 red bird's eye chillies, roughly chopped

1 tablespoon oyster sauce

1 tablespoon shaoxing rice wine

In a small bowl, combine the preserved bean curd and liquid with sugar. Mash and set aside.

Heat half the oil in a wok on high heat. Pour in the stock, add in the water spinach and stir-fry until spinach is slightly wilted. Remove spinach and set aside.

Heat the remaining oil in the wok on high heat until smoking. Add the garlic, chilli, oyster sauce, wine and preserved bean curd mixture. Stir to combine.

Add the water spinach back into the wok and stir-fry until cooked and well covered in sauce. Remove from heat and serve.

Tip: Preserved bean curd is also known as fermented bean curd or fermented tofu. It comes in white and red versions. This recipe uses the white version.

STUFFED BEAN CURD TOPPED WITH SEAFOOD

This popular Happy's dish comes from the genius of Gavin's mum, Linda. While the flavours are simple, the contrasting textures of this dish make it truly special, from the tofu's crispy coating and soft centre, to the pleasing bite of the minced prawns. Diners often order this dish alongside the comparatively pungent water spinach with garlic and chilli, in case you feel like creating a Happy pairing at home.

10 raw tiger prawns, shelled and deveined with tails removed

½ teaspoon salt

½ teaspoon white pepper

1 teaspoon cornflour

450 g firm tofu

vegetable or canola oil, for deep-frying

2 cups cornflour, extra

2 eggs, lightly beaten

SEAFOOD TOPPING

2 tablespoons vegetable oil

5 raw tiger prawns, shelled, deveined and sliced in half lengthwise with tails removed

5 raw scallops, sliced in half lengthways

½ carrot, sliced and cut into flowers, optional

½ cup snow peas, cut into thirds

1 spring onion, cut into 2 cm lengths

2 cm piece fresh ginger, peeled and sliced

2 shitake mushrooms, sliced

1 tablespoon oyster sauce

1 tablespoon shaoxing rice wine

400 ml chicken stock

CORNFLOUR SLURRY

2 teaspoons cornflour mixed with 2 tablespoons water

Blend the prawns in a food processor until a smooth paste forms. Transfer to a metal bowl. Add the salt, pepper and cornflour. Stir to combine. Using one hand, grab the mixture and repeatedly beat against the bowl until mixture develops elasticity.

Cut the tofu into 10 cubes, roughly 1.5 × 1.5 × 2 cm. Arrange the prawn mixture on top of each tofu cube.

Fill a large heavy-based saucepan approximately two-thirds full of oil. Slowly bring to 180°C over medium–high heat. This might take up to 10 minutes. Roll each cube of prawn tofu in the extra cornflour and then coat in the beaten egg. Deep-fry until golden, around 2–3 minutes. Remove and set aside on the serving plate.

To make the seafood topping, heat half the vegetable oil in a wok on high heat, add the seafood and stir-fry until the seafood changes colour. Drain on a plate lined with paper towel.

Heat the remaining oil in the wok on high heat. Add all the vegetables and oyster sauce and then return the seafood to the wok. Toss thoroughly.

Add the stock and then simmer for 1 minute. Add the cornflour slurry and toss until mixture is thickened. Serve the seafood topping poured over the stuffed bean curd.

THE LOST COUSINS OF AUSTRALIAN CHINESE DISHES

Do people in China eat the same dishes that are served in Chinese restaurants in regional Australia? Is sweet and sour pork really Chinese food? The answers are 'kind of' and 'yes'. The origin stories of many classic Australian Chinese dishes can be traced back to Cantonese food.

Most Australian Chinese food is closely related to Cantonese food, because the first Chinese people to arrive in Australia in the mid-1800s were from Canton, a coastal province in the south of China, which these days is known as Guangdong.

The Chinese largely came from the See Yup region in Guangdong (the Four Counties region), and subsequent waves of Chinese immigrants often came from Guangdong and Hong Kong, which led to the distinct Cantonese influence on Australian Chinese food in Chinatowns, suburbs, and regional Australia.

For much of the twentieth century, when you went out for Chinese food in Australia – be it beef and black bean or yum cha – you were most likely eating Cantonese food. This was before the current popularity of other regional Chinese cuisines, such as Shanghainese or Sichuanese.

Here are the origin stories of eight Australian Chinese dishes, which can mostly be traced back to Cantonese cooking...

SPRING ROLLS

Spring rolls are a traditional festival food in China, eaten to celebrate Lunar New Year, which is also known as Spring Festival because it marks the start of spring. They're an auspicious way to welcome the new year because they look like bars of gold. A Chinese proverb says 'One spring roll does not make the season of spring', which can be interpreted as 'Always eat more than one spring roll'. Go on. It would be rude not to.

SALT AND PEPPER SQUID

What some call Australia's national dish has origins in Guangdong. This Cantonese dish is a popular feature in cha chaan tengs (Hong Kong-style diners which serve a mix of Western and Chinese food), open-air food stalls, and restaurants in Hong Kong, Guangdong, and Macau. Other dishes commonly cooked in this salt and pepper style are prawns, pork ribs, and tofu.

SWEET AND SOUR FISH

Sweet and sour fish has been served at banquets in Suzhou in the Jiangsu province of China for more than 200 years. There, it's called squirrel fish: a whole fish is scored and then deep-fried, making the fish look like it has the bushy tail of a squirrel.

LEMON CHICKEN

Lemon chicken is a Cantonese dish that's been served in the cha chaan tengs of Hong Kong since the 1960s, although the version that you'll find at these diners is unlikely to be as brightly coloured yellow as the ones served in Australia.

SWEET AND SOUR PORK

This is probably one of the most well-known Chinese dishes outside China. It's a Cantonese dish, and its origins can be traced back to a menu written in the Tang Dynasty, in 708AD. There are regional variations on this dish, such as the Shanghainese version which uses spare ribs. It's less bright red in colour, and its name translates to 'sugar vinegar spare ribs'. The Hong Kong or Cantonese version uses vinegar, preserved plums, and haw flakes, which are small biscuits made from tart and bright pink hawthorn berries.

DEEP-FRIED ICE CREAM

Perhaps deep-fried ice cream can trace its roots to the Cantonese dish of 'fried fresh milk'. It's also known as deep-fried custard, where jelly-like blocks of cold milk and eggs are battered and deep-fried until golden brown. They are not, however, topped with chocolate, strawberry, or caramel syrup.

PRAWN TOAST

This delightful invention comes from Hong Kong-style English afternoon teas, and is a match made in heaven: deep-fried pairing of a British-style sandwich with wonton filling. In cha chaan tengs in Hong Kong, you can even order prawn toast with a side of thick-cut chips.

SIZZLING MONGOLIAN LAMB

The lost cousin of sizzling Mongolian lamb is stir-fried lamb with spring onions from Beijing. It's said to be made famous by a poet from Fuzhou called Wang Youzhan, who travelled to the northern parts of China in 1920 and returned to his home in south-eastern China and requested that his cook make it for him.

A NEW WAVE

RAYMOND'S AT MALUA BAY

MALUA BAY, NEW SOUTH WALES

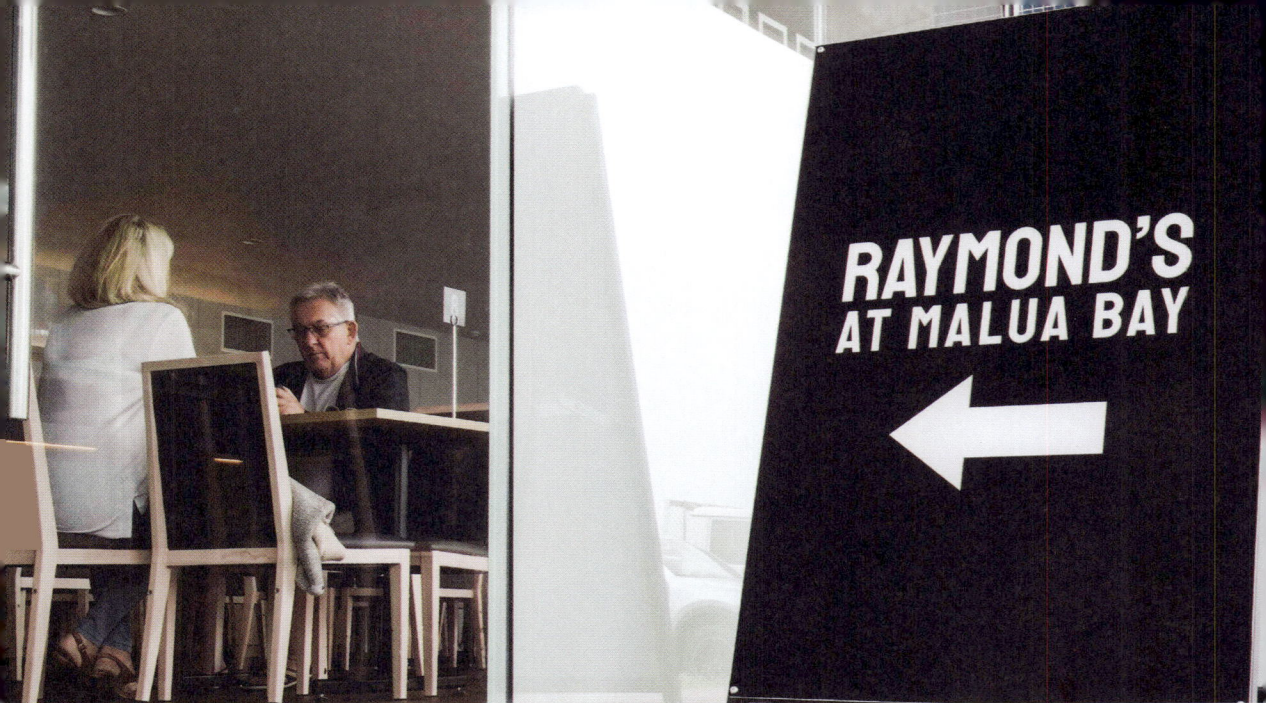

'If you'd asked me as a kid if I'd ever come back to live in Batemans Bay as an adult, I'd say, "A hundred per cent no. Hell no!",' says Emily Ng, who runs Raymond's at Malua Bay with her parents, Raymond and Susie, and her husband, Jonny.

In 2019, Raymond's original restaurant at Malua Bowling Club was destroyed by the Black Summer bushfires, which devastated much of the New South Wales South Coast. Susie, who was in her late sixties, saw this as a wonderful opportunity for her and Raymond to retire and move to Sydney to be near their grandchildren. But Raymond, then 75, secretly began looking for a new location for their next restaurant. 'He couldn't bear to let the fire take his restaurant,' says Susie.

The sleek new restaurant opened in 2020, right on the beach. The modern decor, designed by Raymond and Susie's son, Cameron, is so different from a typical old-school Chinese restaurant, that people have mistaken it for a cafe and come in asking for coffee.

And so Emily, tired of doing her digital marketing job from home in Sydney during Covid ('The working from home, the conference calls – the novelty wore off very quickly'), decided to move to Malua Bay to help her parents.

Raymond, formerly a tailor in Hong Kong, opened the original Raymond's Chinese restaurant in Batemans Bay in 1989, before moving to the Malua Bay Bowling Club in 2008. 'When I arrived in Australia, I had to learn another trade, because Australians don't really wear suits,' he says. After so many years in the area, and as the only Chinese restaurant in the town of 2000 people, Raymond's has become a much-loved institution for everyone from local lawn bowlers to holidaymakers. 'Everyone loves Raymond,' jokes Susie. Even martial arts legend Jackie Chan has dined at Raymond's, to enjoy some home-style Cantonese cooking on his travels.

Diners come for the honey prawns, made with local honey from nearby Mogo, where the bees work a winter flowering tree called the spotted gum. In another nod to local produce, you can order oysters from Batemans Bay, which grow in an area that's 98 per cent state forest and national parks, and are fed by the Tasman sea.

Occasionally, there are specials on the menu like Peking duck served with Raymond's homemade hoisin sauce. And if you bring in a local lobster, Raymond will fry it up with ginger, garlic, and spring onions. Meanwhile, Emily has been adding to the range of deep-fried ice cream options, with new toppings such as Nutella and Lotus Biscoff.

Working with her parents means that Emily now spends more time with them than she ever did before. When Emily was growing up, her parents spent most of their time at the restaurant. 'Mum and Dad would always call at about seven and they'd go, "What do you want for dinner?" And me and my brother would place our orders. And then the doorbell would ring, and a takeaway box would appear, but Mum and Dad would be gone. It was incredible. And that was every night,' says Emily.

'I'd have Caucasian friends and Mum would let me stay at their houses on the weekend. And they'd eat dinner at the table. So civilised, like tablecloth, placemats and knife and fork laid out. And I was like, "Wow. What is this?"'

These days, now that Emily runs the restaurant, she has a better understanding of how her parents spent their time. 'It's a whole different ball game to look after staffing, management, to make sure the business is running smoothly.'

She gets up at 7 am and goes to the gym, heads home for breakfast, and then arrives at the restaurant at 10.15 am where she checks the stock. When Raymond arrives at the restaurant, he lets Emily know if there's anything he needs, like paying bills. She has lunch at 11 am and the lunch shift begins at 11.30 am. At 2.45 pm, when lunch finishes, she cashes up and cleans up, and has an hour break, where she might drive up to Batemans Bay to pick up oysters from the oyster shed. At 5 pm she has dinner, and the dinner shift starts at 5.30 pm and goes until 8.30 or 9 pm, before it's time to cash up and clean up again. 'I have Mondays off, but usually I spend those doing accounts. The days roll into one,' says Emily. 'But I also get to sit at the beach and look at the ocean, and it's not a bad place to be.'

For Emily, one of the most important things now is seeing how happy her Dad is. 'I know it seems like we work really hard, but he's just so happy. He's healthy. And also just hearing the customers say, "This is honestly the best Chinese food we've ever eaten." I never got that type of satisfaction from my old job. Not once. I never got the fulfilment I do now. And I knew I would regret it for the rest of my life if I didn't take this opportunity now.'

HONEY PRAWNS

Is it even an Australian Chinese restaurant if honey prawns aren't on the menu? Crisp, golden, and sweet on the outside; soft and savoury on the inside: these honey prawns taste of the land and the ocean in every bite. Honey prawns are a delicious example of a Westernised style of Chinese food: cooking that has been made sweeter for the Western palate. Raymond uses local honey from the nearby town of Mogo to make his honey prawns extra special.

340 g raw king prawns, shelled and devained with tails removed
1 teaspoon chicken powder
½ teaspoon salt
½ teaspoon pepper
vegetable or canola oil, for deep-frying
2 teaspoons sesame seeds

BATTER

1 tablespoon cornflour
3 tablespoons self-raising flour
1 tablespoon plain flour
1 tablespoon custard powder

HONEY SAUCE

1 cup honey
¼ cup store-bought lemon sauce
¼ cup sugar
¼ cup white vinegar

Combine the prawns, chicken powder, salt and pepper in a medium bowl.

To make the batter, combine all batter ingredients in a large bowl and add water until the batter is thick enough to coat the back of a spoon.

Fill a wok or large pan with oil approximately two-thirds full. Slowly bring to 180°C over medium–high heat. This might take up to 10 minutes. Using tongs or wooden chopsticks, dip each prawn in the batter and drop gently into the hot oil. Deep-fry prawns until golden, then remove using a slotted spoon and drain on a plate lined with paper towel or a strainer.

To make the honey sauce, combine all the ingredients for sauce in a wok or large pan on high heat. Cook until bubbling, then bring it to a simmer.

Add deep-fried prawns. Stir-fry until the prawns are covered with sauce. Serve garnished with sesame seeds.

SIZZLING MONGOLIAN LAMB

While the sounds of sizzling Mongolian lamb are hard to replicate at home, the flavours are definitely doable. The easy-to-make Mongolian sauce also goes well with beef, chicken, seafood, and your favourite combination of vegetables and tofu. While the origins of this dish are varied, one story traces it to a dish of stir-fried lamb with spring onions that a Fujianese poet called Wang Youzhan ate in Beijing in 1920. When he returned home to Fuzhou, he asked his cook to make it for him.

4 tablespoons vegetable oil

340 g lamb backstrap, cut into 1 cm-thick slices

½ medium onion, finely sliced

½ leek, white part only, finely sliced

2 garlic cloves, finely diced

MONGOLIAN SAUCE

2 tablespoons hoisin sauce

2 tablespoons plum sauce

2 tablespoons barbecue sauce

2 tablespoons ground bean sauce

2 tablespoons chilli bean sauce

To make the Mongolian sauce, combine all sauce ingredients in a medium bowl.

In a wok or large pan, heat 2 tablespoons of vegetable oil, add the lamb and stir-fry until golden. Remove the lamb and set aside.

Heat 1 tablespoon of remaining oil in the wok or pan and stir-fry the onion and leek for a few minutes, until they start to soften. Remove onion mixture and set aside.

Add the remaining tablespoon of oil to the wok or pan and add the garlic. Fry for 30 seconds until fragrant, then add the Mongolian sauce. Once the sauce is hot, return the lamb and the onion mixture to the pan. Stir-fry until everything is coated well with sauce.

COMBINATION FRIED RICE

Ah, fried rice. The perfect side dish, and also a complete meal in its own right. Consider this recipe as simply a guide – you can use any combination of cooked meats, and also substitute the meat for carrot, peas, and corn to make the dish vegetarian. Raymond's version here is very close to the most famous type of fried rice – Yangzhou fried rice – which is from Jiangsu, a coastal province north of Shanghai. It's also made with barbecued pork and prawns. Make sure that your ingredients are dry to ensure that your rice fries up nicely without excess moisture.

2 tablespoons vegetable oil
1 egg
200 g char siu (Chinese barbecued pork)
50 g cooked, shredded chicken breast
50 g ham, finely chopped
10 shelled cooked prawns
2 cups cooked white jasmine rice
1 spring onion, chopped

SAUCE

2 tablespoons light soy sauce
1 teaspoon chicken powder
1 teaspoon sugar
½ teaspoon salt

To make the sauce, combine the sauce ingredients in a small bowl.

In a wok or large pan, heat 1 tablespoon of oil and scramble the egg. Remove the egg and set aside.

Heat the remaining tablespoon of oil in the wok or pan and stir-fry the pork, chicken, ham and prawns. Add the rice and mix thoroughly, breaking up any large clumps.

Add the sauce and mix well to combine. Add the scrambled egg and toss together.

Add the spring onion and toss together, then serve.

CHINESE RESTAURANT
BINGO

**LUCKY CAT**	**NAPKIN IN WINE GLASS**	**DOUBLE HAPPINESS**	**VINYL CHAIRS**
**HIGH CHAIR** (THAT THE RESTAURANT'S KIDS GREW UP WITH)	**PHOENIX**	**CIRCULAR ENTRANCE**	**LUCKY BAMBOO**
**PAPER DOILIES**	**PAGODA ROOF OR ENTRANCE**	**SCALLOPED CURTAINS**	**THE WORDS 'LUCKY, GOLDEN, PALACE, DYNASTY, OR DRAGON'**
**LONGEVITY**	**KENNY G OR RICHARD CLAYDERMAN MUSIC**	**CHINESE VASE**	**PRAWN CHIPS**

What makes a quintessential Chinese restaurant in regional Australia? It's more than just sweet and sour pork and deep-fried ice cream. Observant diners may argue it's not an old-school Chinese restaurant without the following features. How many can you spot in your favourite?

WHITE LACE CURTAINS	**RED CHINESE KNOTS**	**GOLDFISH**	**CORNINGWARE PLATES**
THREE LUCKY GODS	**ROSE GARNISH MADE OF CARROT**	**LAZY SUSAN**	**LUCK**
OLD-SCHOOL FONT	**OCTAGONAL WINDOWS**	**CHINESE PAINTINGS**	**WOOD-PANELLED WALLS**
NAPKIN AS CROWN	**LAMINATED TABLECLOTH**	**RED LANTERNS**	**DRAGON**

HAPPY GARDEN

DARWIN, NORTHERN TERRITORY

At Darwin institution Happy Garden, dishes on the menu tell the story of the Lee family, who opened the restaurant only six months after the family arrived in Australia from Portugal in 1981. It was a long journey for this Hakka family from their home of East Timor.

Hakka means 'guest families', and refers to a subgroup of Chinese people who fled northern parts of China in the Qing dynasty (1636–1911) because of invasions and unrest. They then settled in the southern parts of China, like Guangdong in the Lees' case, and migrated around the world. It's said that everywhere they go, they're guests, not locals. 'For me, I've always said that we've actually lived a Hakka life,' says Jason, who runs Happy Garden with his brother Daniel. 'Our great-grandparents left China. My parents were born in Timor.'

In East Timor, Jason and Daniel's parents had nine children and they were very successful. 'We had two rice fields, a cattle station, and 99 cows, apparently,' says Jason. 'And there was a bit of a variety store that sold anything from sugar and coffee to shoes. It even sold fuel,' adds Daniel. 'It was kind of like a one-stop shop.'

One Happy Garden dish that tells the story of the Lees' time in Timor is their famous tamarind chicken wings, which are sweet and tangy, and sticky from the tamarind. 'This is Timorese street food,' says Jason. 'Every Timorese Chinese barbecue that you go to, you've got the tamarind sauce to go on your satay or barbecued meat.' The Lees had tamarind trees in their backyard in Maliana, and would often pick the fruit from the tree to eat.

The Lee family's life in East Timor was cut short by the country's civil war in 1975. 'It came around pretty suddenly. We didn't have much time to prepare. So we left with just a Land Cruiser, not many belongings, and negotiated to drive into West Timor, which is on the border of Indonesia,' says Jason.

Because East Timor was a colony of Portugal at that time, the Lees were able to go there as refugees. They stayed there for five-and-a-half years. Although the family didn't speak much of the local language, they still managed to embrace the tastes of Portugal, which is reflected today in their popular chicken and potato dish. 'It's simple and it's got a bit of that peppery taste to it,' says Jason. 'The potatoes are the influence from the Portuguese. For us, this is Portuguese Timorese Hakka fusion, something we have at home with the kids.'

The Lees were able to come to Australia from Portugal because of then Prime Minister Malcolm Fraser's family reunification policy. 'My uncle, my mum's brother, sponsored us,' says Daniel. 'It was difficult, because my mum had ten children, and that doesn't fit the definition of the normal Australian family.'

'The policy was quite generous, and allowed us to come. Our aim was always to come to Australia. So we were quite happy to come here. We never looked back.' Not long after they arrived in Darwin, Jason and Daniel's mum started working at a fish and chip shop in Parap.

'One day, the lady who owned a fish and chip shop asked my dad, "I want to sell my business. You've got a lot of children. Why don't you buy my business?"' says Jason.

In the beginning, Happy Garden served old-school fish and chips alongside Chinese takeaway. But a few years later, in an effort to increase the business, it expanded into a fully fledged restaurant with more than 120 dishes. And these days, they have four other Happy Garden restaurants around Darwin, and employ more than fifty staff.

Most of the dishes on the menu reflect the Lees' Hakka and Cantonese roots, like braised pork belly with preserved mustard greens, eggplant with minced pork, and salt and pepper tofu. The restaurant also makes its own barbecued meats Cantonese style: char siu, roast duck, and roast pork. Keeping with the spirit of multi-ethnic Darwin, Happy Garden also explores many non-Chinese Asian flavours, like Malaysian chilli prawns, which were added to the menu in 2007. Their roast pork laksa is the happy marriage between the Lees' Cantonese identity and Darwin's proud title as the laksa capital of Australia. 'My wife was actually born in Penang, and her cousin introduced a chef that wanted to come to Australia, so we sponsored him,' says Jason. 'Throughout history we've had chefs that come from Taiwan, Hong Kong, and various parts of the world. They bring us their experience and share it with us. And some of it stays with us still, even though they may have moved on.'

At Happy Garden, the Lees' cooking reflects the flavours of their long journey from East Timor to Portugal to Darwin. They've created quite the legacy in Darwin, and the next generation is thinking about legacy too, taking that even further. 'My dad has the dream of franchising the business and having lots of stores around Australia. I'd love to help him make that happen,' says Jason's son, Nathan, who's currently studying at the University of Melbourne.

Gone are the days of the Lees being Hakka 'guest families' passing through town. They're home.

TAMARIND CHICKEN WINGS

Every family has their own version of tamarind sauce in Timor-Leste, where tamarind grows prolifically. The Lees had tamarind trees in their backyard in Maliana, and would often pick the fruit from the tree to eat. This thick, dark, sweet and tangy sauce is typically used to baste lamb satays cooked over coals in the markets, but it's great on all types of meats.

800 g chicken wings, with wings and drumettes separated

1 teaspoon sugar

1 teaspoon salt

¼ teaspoon white pepper

1 garlic clove, grated

1 teaspoon shaoxing rice wine or dry sherry

3 tablespoons cornflour

1 tablespoon flour

vegetable or canola oil, for deep-frying

sliced fresh chilli, to serve

sliced spring onion, to serve

TAMARIND SAUCE

MAKES AROUND 2 LITRES

400 g (1 block) tamarind

1 tablespoon canola oil or neutral tasting oil

2 onions, diced

2 stems lemongrass, white part only, bruised and sliced

4–6 garlic cloves, bruised

1 tablespoon white pepper

1¾ kg sugar

620 ml bottle kecap manis

The purpose of this first step is to separate the tamarind pulp from the fibrous and fleshy seeds, to extract the tamarind puree which forms the base of this sauce.

In a large saucepan, bring 2.5 litres of water to the boil. Break apart the tamarind block and add it to the water. Simmer for 30 minutes.

Place a fine mesh sieve over a large bowl and strain the liquid through the sieve, using a large spoon to squeeze as much puree out as possible. Discard seeds.

There should be approximately two litres of strained tamarind puree at the end of the process.

To make the sauce, add the oil, onion and lemongrass to a heavy saucepan on medium–high heat, and stir-fry until fragrant. Add garlic and tamarind puree. Bring to the boil then reduce heat and simmer until the sauce is reduced to about two-thirds, around 90 minutes, skimming any scum on the surface.

Add pepper, sugar and kecap manis and simmer for around 45 minutes to an hour, until the sauce is thick and glossy.

The sauce can be stored in sterilised jars in the fridge, where they can be kept for up to three months.

In a large bowl, combine wings with sugar, salt, pepper, garlic and cooking wine. Cover and set aside for around 30 minutes.

Toss wings in cornflour, then coat in flour.

Fill a large wok or saucepan approximately two-thirds full with oil. Slowly bring to 180°C over medium–high heat. This might take up to 10 minutes. Fry the wings in batches until golden and crispy. Drain on a plate lined with paper towel.

Heat a cup of the tamarind sauce in a wok or frying pan on medium heat, and add wings and toss. Add more sauce as required to ensure the chicken wings are coated thickly.

Serve sprinkled with sliced chilli and sliced spring onion.

SWEET AND SOUR BARRAMUNDI

At Happy Garden, wild caught barramundi fillets take pride of place in this tangy dish, but you can use any firm white fish fillet like snapper, whiting, or ling. The sweet and sour sauce, which is a little more sour than sweet, hasn't changed since the restaurant first opened in 1981. Make this at home, and you'll be dining similarly to banquet goers 200 years ago in Jiangsu, a coastal province north of Shanghai, where sweet and sour fish originated.

300 g barramundi fillets, cut into thick slices
1 cup cornflour
vegetable or canola oil, for deep-frying
¼ cup finely diced onion
1 carrot, finely diced
¼ cup finely diced capsicum
¼ cup canned and drained pineapple pieces, finely diced
small handful curly parsley, to garnish, optional
carrot flower, to garnish, optional

SWEET AND SOUR SAUCE

1 cup water
¼ cup white vinegar
1/3 cup sugar
1/3 cup tomato sauce
juice of ½ lemon, optional

CORNFLOUR SLURRY

1 tablespoon cornflour mixed with 1 tablespoon water

To make the sweet and sour sauce, combine sauce ingredients in a small saucepan and bring to the boil. Simmer for 5 minutes. Add cornflour slurry and simmer for a further minute until thickened.

Fill a large heavy-based saucepan approximately two-thirds full with oil. Slowly bring to 180°C over medium–high heat. This might take up to 10 minutes. Pat dry the barramundi and lightly toss in cornflour. Deep-fry fish in batches until lightly golden. The fish should float to the top of the oil when done. Drain fish in a colander or on a wire rack.

Heat a wok or saucepan on high heat, then add one tablespoon of oil and stir-fry the onion, carrot and capsicum for 1 minute. The vegetables should still retain some crunch. Add the sweet and sour sauce, pineapple and fish, and stir-fry for 1 minute.

CHICKEN AND POTATOES

This comfort food – a firm favourite for Happy Garden customers – was created by the Mama of Happy Garden, Mrs Nu Ling Lee, in a nod to her family's time in Portugal. It takes ingredients commonly used in Portuguese dishes – such as chicken and potatoes – and combines them with Chinese flavours – like soy sauce and shaoxing wine – to create a deep-fried potato stir-fried with tender chicken pieces. It's finished with a savoury and peppery sauce.

300 g chicken thigh fillets, sliced

½ teaspoon salt

1 teaspoon sugar

1 tablespoon light soy sauce

1 tablespoon dry sherry or shaoxing rice wine

vegetable or canola oil, for deep-frying

4–6 potatoes (up to 500 g), peeled and cubed

1 tablespoon vegetable or canola oil, extra

2 garlic cloves, roughly chopped

⅓ cup frozen peas

¾ cup chicken stock

white pepper, to taste

tomato, cucumber and curly parsley, to garnish, optional

SAUCE

2 tablespoons oyster sauce

½ tablespoon sugar

2 teaspoons light soy sauce

½ teaspoon dark soy sauce

CORNFLOUR SLURRY

1 tablespoon cornflour mixed with 1 tablespoon water

In a large bowl, combine chicken with salt, sugar, light soy sauce, and cooking wine. Cover and place in the fridge for 30 minutes.

Fill a wok or large heavy-based saucepan approximately two-thirds full with oil. Slowly bring to 180°C over medium–high heat. This might take up to 10 minutes. Fry potatoes in batches until golden and cooked through. Drain on a plate lined with paper towel.

In a wok or large saucepan, heat the extra oil and add the garlic cloves and chicken. Stir-fry for 3 minutes until the chicken changes colour.

Add potatoes, sauce mixture, and frozen peas and stir-fry for 2–3 minutes. Add chicken stock and a couple of grinds of white pepper. Add cornflour slurry and stir-fry for another minute.

BOK CHOY AND CHINESE MUSHROOMS

Master this classic Chinese way of cooking vegetables, and you'll be eating restaurant-quality dishes at home in no time. Use different types of mushrooms to change it up: wood ear, shimeji, enoki, or oyster mushrooms also work well in this dish. Taste the sauce and adjust the seasoning as necessary. It's ok to add more oyster sauce or soy sauce or sugar depending on what flavours you need more of. Another tip for adjustments: If the sauce is too thin, add more cornflour slurry. And if it's too thick, add more of the water you used to soak the mushrooms.

50 g whole dried shiitake mushrooms

6 bunches bok choy

2 tablespoons vegetable or canola oil

2 garlic cloves, finely chopped

dash of dry sherry or shaoxing rice wine

a few drops of sesame oil, to serve

SAUCE

1½ tablespoons oyster sauce

1 tablespoon light soy sauce

¼ teaspoon dark soy sauce

¼ teaspoon salt

1 teaspoon sugar

CORNFLOUR SLURRY

1 tablespoon cornflour mixed with 1 tablespoon water

Soak mushrooms in two cups of warm water for 30 minutes or until soft (depends on the thickness of the mushrooms). Drain, reserve the water, and cut the stalks off the mushrooms.

To make the sauce, mix the sauce ingredients in a small bowl.

Cut and discard the base of the bok choy. Wash the stems well and slice on the diagonal, separating the leaves and the stems. Slice the bigger leaves in half.

Heat half the vegetable oil in a wok or large saucepan to medium to high heat. Add bok choy and stir-fry for 2 minutes, then place in a bowl.

In the same wok, add remaining tablespoon of oil and the garlic and fry until fragrant, around 10 seconds or so. Add the mushrooms and stir-fry, then add about ½ of the strained reserved mushroom water and bring to a simmer.

Add the sauce mixture and a dash of cooking wine, then simmer for approximately 5 minutes. Add cornflour slurry and stir for 1 minute until thickened. Add a few drops of sesame oil to finish. Serve mushrooms over bok choy.

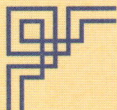

A LOVE FOR ALL THINGS
RETRO CHINESE

Chinese food brings back a lot of wonderful memories for me. It feels safe, comfy and familiar, and as I've gotten older I've grown to appreciate the interior design and aesthetic of the restaurants. The gold accents, fish tanks, wallpaper, the beautiful lantern-style light fittings, plastic roses ... I am in love with it all.

I started @Retro.Chinese.Restaurants on Instagram in 2018 and it now has more than 3800 followers. I suppose I knew deep down I wasn't the only person addicted to retro Chinese food and style, and I was right!

These days my favourites are my two locals: Three Sisters BBQ in Katoomba and Ho's Palace in Blackheath. They are both excellent in their own way. Three Sisters BBQ is a small, low-key, family-run place, complete with a daughter who does her homework up the back of the dining room. Ho's Palace is a much larger, garish and kitschy example of Asian-style maximalism, run by husband and wife team, Sam and Aileen Ho, which opened in 1986. Both are worth visiting if you're ever in the Blue Mountains!

KELLY PARSONS

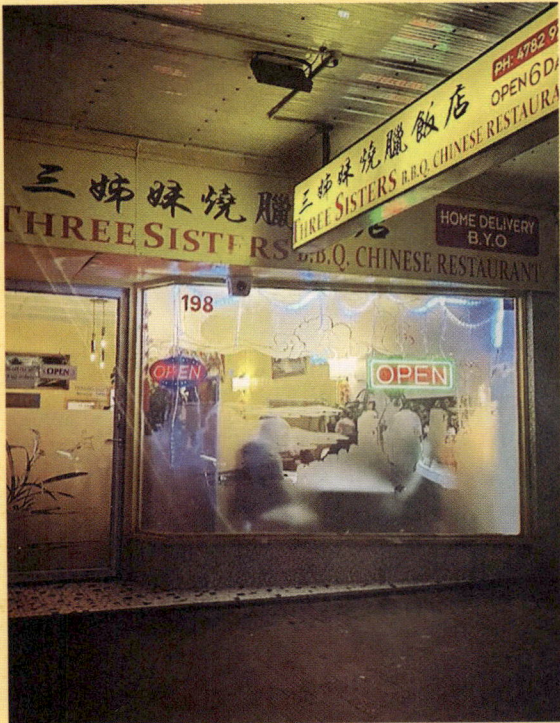

MEMORIES FROM AROUND AUSTRALIA

1970s–1980s

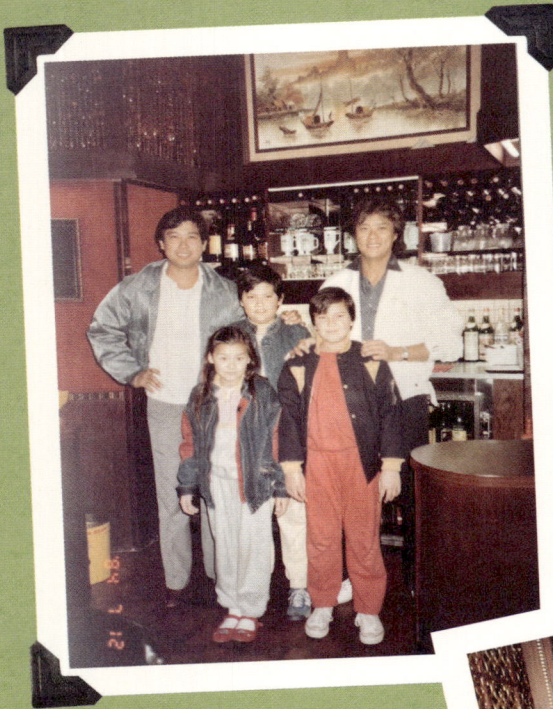

The Ho Wah Restaurant in Newcastle, New South Wales was established in the 1970s by my grandfather on my dad's side. I still recall my first visit to Hong Kong as a child thinking the place actually smelt like our restaurant! Many nights I was kept awake by the rattling of mahjong tiles and adult exclamations of games won and lost, along with the sing-song of Cantonese banter. Even though I've seen it made from scratch I still marvel at how fried ice cream works. My sister is right, though – caramel sauce, not canned fruit salad, is the proper accompaniment to eat it with.

DERREN LOWE

In the 1970s and '80s our parents would regularly take us, their three kids and subsequent grandchildren, to the Chinese restaurants in Beverly Hills in Sydney. There were several of them, and over time a couple of them became quite 'classy' with the tables covered in white tablecloths. There were cloth serviettes, wine glasses, and waiters dressed in dinner suits. One evening, as my father was preparing to leave for an evening out dressed in his dinner suit, his five-year-old granddaughter said, 'Is Grandpa going to work at the Chinese restaurant?'

JUDITH HARLEY

My parents, Rosa and Gee (Fred) Wing, owned Wing Yuen Restaurant at Tunstall Square in Doncaster East, Victoria for about eighteen years. I guess our restaurant became most famous for Dad's homemade dim sims. People would travel far and wide just for the dim sims! Tuesday was dim-sim-making day. Grandma and Uncle James would travel by bus from the city every week to help make the twenty-five dozen or so dim sims. Dad, to this day, still makes them – but just for the family (sorry!). We now have a dim-sim-making day every couple of months which is so much fun, with Dad doing the quality control and checking that they're the right size: 'Not too big, otherwise you won't make a profit!'

LISA ADDERLY

Bookmarked through my life was going to the Sing Wah Chinese Restaurant in my hometown of Tenterfield, New South Wales. We celebrated every occasion at the Sing Wah. Birthdays, anniversaries, graduations. And because of this, Chinese food will never not taste nostalgic and special. It was so different from what we ate at home, and was such a welcome break from steak and vegetables, sausages and vegetables, chicken and vegetables. Sing Wah was where I was introduced to Mum's favourite chicken and cashew nut, garlic king prawns, and my favourite: short soup. You could say I've been a short soup fan for a long time. And that's the long and short (soup) of it.

LUKE TRIBE

As a teenager, growing up in Carlingford in north-west Sydney, I used to babysit for the owners of a local Chinese restaurant. Unfortunately, I don't remember the restaurant's name, but every Saturday night without fail they would bring me home the leftovers from the restaurant – a pile of takeaway containers topped by a mountain of prawn crackers. I would arrive home, three doors down the road, where my parents would be in bed waiting for me to get back from babysitting. And there we would sit, having a Chinese food picnic in their bed at midnight, scoffing spring rolls, and dim sims with abandon! Best babysitting job I ever had.

ANN-MARIE LOEBEL

My parents owned and operated the Boonah Chinese Restaurant in Queensland for twenty years. They moved to Australia from Hong Kong in the early '80s, lured by the promise of a better lifestyle, good work, and money. My dad, who had worked in construction in Hong Kong, learned the restaurant trade and how to cook Western Chinese food upon arriving in Australia from his brother who was already based in New South Wales.

Everything at our restaurant was made fresh by hand, so the day started early for my dad and mum, and ended late. We would come in and help when we were ready for the day. Us kids were independent from a young age, and we managed to look after ourselves and each other, and would also help in the restaurant.

As we grew older, we progressed from peeling spring roll wrappers to making spring rolls, dim sums, wiping glasses, cutting vegetables, taking orders, and serving customers – there was always something to do. I loved when we had our naps in the restaurant by pulling chairs together to make a bed and turning on the air conditioning – there was no air con at home and Boonah got pretty hot in summer!

Despite the long hours and daily monotony of running a restaurant, my parents were determined to keep the business going to provide for our family and send us all to private school. I am grateful for the lessons and values that I learned growing up in a Chinese restaurant. It taught me independence, strong family values, work ethics, perseverance, and the motivation and determination to dream big and do better. I will always treasure the memories of our family days on Mondays, yum cha in Chinatown, and even a brush with fame when Jason Donovan and Peter Phelps came in to order takeaway.

LILY MA

My dad, Sidney Wu, came to Australia from Hong Kong in 1975 as a sponsored migrant. He worked in Sydney restaurants then moved to, and managed, the Parkes RSL club with my mum, Anita Wu, before starting their own business, the Oceania Chinese Restaurant in Broken Hill, New South Wales in 1982.

The red brick facade, circular windows, and interior arches were technical challenges the local builders took on with great pride. My parents attended to every detail from kitchen equipment, menu design, crockery and cutlery, silk uniforms, wallpaper, and artwork, through to making sure the Chinese chefs and their families stayed at our family home to save on rent and to feel secure. It was an ambitious announcement of Chinese culture in an outback Australian town – not a small affair whatsoever. My brother and I were horrified that our parents needed to drain our teeny savings account for this seemingly risky venture.

The Oceania attracted everyone from families, executives, hip types, drunken teenagers, travellers, to people marking special occasions, seeking a quick takeaway, through to glamorous international film stars and crews. I was alarmed to learn on one occasion that my warm-hearted mum turned away a very polite, fur-draped Dynasty star during a busy Friday evening dinner service because she didn't have a reservation! 'Fair is fair, there is nothing I can do,' Mum said to me.

CATHERINE WU

When I was a kid, at the age of around six in 1977, I was aware of a distinction between an outside life and an inside life. The outside life was school and the inside life was family. The two very rarely mixed. I even used different languages in each of these worlds. I spoke English at school and Cantonese everywhere else. After school, I would quickly do my homework and then go with my parents to the restaurant – the Say Kong Cafe in Wentworthville, New South Wales – at 4.30 pm, ready for service at 5 pm. The restaurant had red and gold flocked wallpaper and heavy silk curtains, green for summer, orange for winter. This is the Chinese restaurant I remember.

At first, I'd sit on the bags of food, heaping sacks of rice, breadcrumbs, and flour, watching my parents do their thing. I fell asleep quite a lot, and was lulled and comforted by the rapping of Dad's cooking utensils on his wok (it sounded like mahjong tiles!), the creak of the door in between the kitchen and the dining room. Then as I got older, I helped make food, and I became an expert at wrapping spring rolls and pressing prawn cutlets. Finally, when I was tall enough, I helped out in the dining room, taking orders, making drinks and serving meals. I didn't mind. I spent a lot of time with my mum and dad. I loved that.

FREYA SU

Having served four generations of customers over the course of forty years, my parents are the owners of Yee's Chinese Cuisine located in the small country town of Branxton, New South Wales. Originally, Yee's restaurant opened in the early 1980s and was operating out of the Workers Club in Greta, New South Wales. In 1993, my dad bought his own space in Branxton to run their restaurant, where they are still located today.

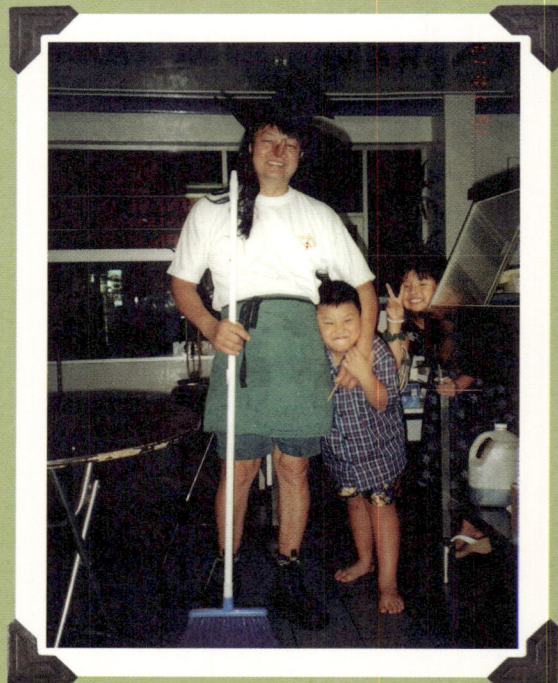

A family-run Chinese restaurant can be a place of mixed emotions. While there is plenty of joy and a true sense of community, there is also a layer of otherness and racial abuse sprinkled throughout the decades of my parents running their restaurant, and in mine and my siblings' lives as Asian kids growing up in a town that had a population of roughly ten to fifteen Asian people. Feelings of community, friendship, dissonance, stress, recovery, freedom, anxiety, anger, stability, and joy can exist all at once.

Although some moments can feel like a kick in the gut, they have put a fire underneath us that fuels our resilience.

STEFFIE YEE

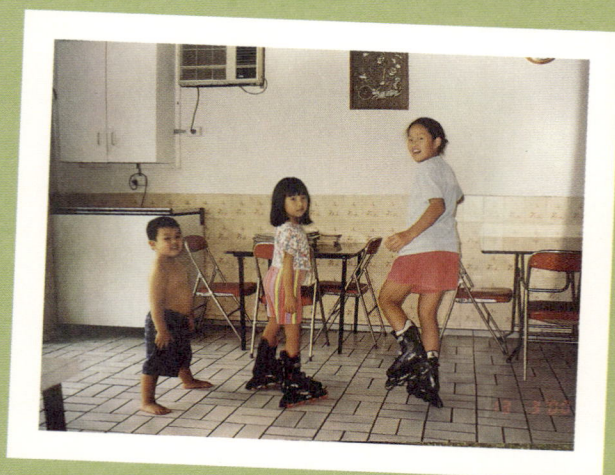

I literally grew up in the Hong Kong Restaurant in Casino, New South Wales, which my parents took over in 1985. I say literally grew up there because I do remember my baby cot in the kitchen as my parents worked during the night, through to being in primary and high school studying under the dull yellow glow of the dining room lights nearly every night.

Being a restaurant kid probably instilled a good, hard work ethic, as seen in many migrant families. Not only were you expected to work hard academically during the week, but you were also expected to physically work hard in the kitchen at nights, and prepare the dining room and food during the weekends!

Because it was a family business I got to see my parents working hard every day and night, so I feel the key thing I learned was to work hard – I saw my parents work hard, sweating in front of the kitchen stoves and wok burners all day, every day.

Since we were only one of maybe three Asian families in Casino back then, we were a close family unit and I do feel lucky to have spent so much time with them and my brother, really contributing to the family.

A benefit of being a restaurant kid, and being one of the rare Asians in a country town back then, was that most townspeople knew who you were and other kids usually treated you fairly well – either because country people are usually nice people or because they liked your food!

HENRY KO

My dad, uncles, and grandpa built Lwoy's Chinese Restaurant in Derby, Western Australia, which opened in 1981. It is now run by Mum and Dad. The restaurant was a second home for myself, two older sisters, and younger brother.

When we were older, Mum would leave us at home more. Sometimes she'd call and tell us dinner was ready and we'd walk together to the restaurant. We had a specific family table reserved for us there. Us kids would set the table as if we were eating at home (with chopsticks and small bowls, of course). Customers would look on curiously when our food came out – it was never what was on the menu. Dad cooked more traditional style dishes for us (less gravy, more vegetables and never sweet and sour pork!).

Each of us kids have had varying degrees of involvement (and remuneration) in the business. We did lots of restaurant 'chores' as kids, such as wrapping plastic sporks with napkins, laundering endless piles of tea towels and tablecloths, doing the dishes when it was really busy, peeling onions and carrots, counting the till, setting and packing up at market stalls, making spring rolls and satay sticks, restocking drinks, taking phone orders, typing up the menus before we knew about word formatting…like trying to figure out how many full stops do you need to line up the pricing just right!?

KING YIN LUI

Toy's Restaurant was my introduction to the world of Chinese restaurants. Indeed, it was my introduction to restaurants. As a six-year-old, I believed that Toy's was the height of sophistication (and, in many ways, in Horsham of the mid-1970s, it was!). Above all, I remember the chopsticks. Each set of Leon's chopsticks came in a paper envelope emblazoned with golden-coloured Chinese characters and simple images of Chinese warriors. I wanted desperately to master the use of chopsticks. Looking back, I suspect that I wanted to show off, so that when Leon or May Har asked the table, 'Chopsticks or fork?', I could say 'Chopsticks'. To help me learn, Leon offered to let me keep his chopsticks, and over a few years, I collected quite a few pairs from Toy's. For a six-year-old who never left the district, this was magical.

ROBERT HEATH

OPEN SESAME (PRAWN TOAST)

DUNSBOROUGH CHINESE RESTAURANT

DUNSBOROUGH, WESTERN AUSTRALIA

Dunsborough Chinese is the most western Chinese restaurant in Australia, not because of its food, but because of its location. Dunsborough is a coastal town of around 7000 people, which is three hours' drive (around 250 kilometres) south of Perth. It's en route to the Margaret River wine region, and is known for its stunning beaches.

You'll find Dunsborough Chinese and its iconic shopfront just off the roundabout at Caves Road, where it's attached to a Coles Express, in a rare display of Chinese-architecture-meets-Australian-petrol-station. Once you step through the grand, Taiwanese-made arches into the restaurant and hear French pianist Richard Clayderman's easy listening tunes on the sound system, you'll forget that you're about to eat just metres away from people filling up their utes.

The restaurant was started by Tom Wu's brother, David, in the 1980s – its original location was nearby – who ran it until his retirement in December 2019 when Tom took over. For a small restaurant, its decor stands out: a giant porcelain Chinese cabbage for luck, an altar in the corner of the restaurant honouring the guardian deity Guan Gong with oranges and burnt incense, and a ten-year-old bonsai bougainvillea, evidence of Tom's bonsai hobby. On each table, small salt and pepper shakers lean against a jug of soy sauce, anticipating a diner's every need.

Before taking on Dunsborough Chinese, Tom worked for eighteen years at his own Chinese restaurant in Australind, a coastal town an hour north of Dunsborough. He sold it in 2006 and worked in Perth until moving to Dunsborough in 2019, happy to return to a small town. It's a trade he got into begrudgingly, at the insistence of a sixty-three-year-old Singaporean chef he met while delivering Asian groceries in Perth in 1978. He'd just arrived in Australia, and he was twenty-three.

Tom left his home of Bạc Liêu in Vietnam because of the war and took a boat from Vietnam to Malaysia. He was on the boat for three days, and then stayed in a refugee camp in Malaysia for three months before arriving in Perth. 'The Singaporean chef said to me, "If you learn to cook, one day you can have your own restaurant"' says Tom. 'But I didn't want to. It was a profession where you never saw the light of day, and daytime is often the busiest.'

Eventually the chef convinced Tom to let him teach him. 'He was so good to me, even though I couldn't hold a wok properly when I first started,' says Tom. 'He taught me every skill patiently until I learned it. We worked our way up from chicken chow mein to stir-fried vermicelli.'

Six months after their lessons together, the Singaporean chef let Tom cook a lunch shift by himself. 'I was very happy,' he says. Over the years, Tom lost touch with the chef. 'I miss him a lot. It is one of my greatest regrets that I didn't see my teacher again before he died,' he says.

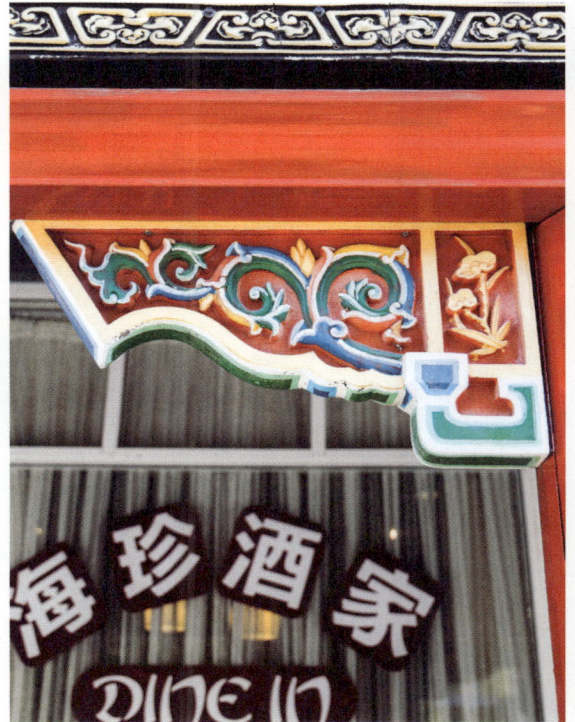

海珍酒家
DINE IN

One of the ways that Tom had to adapt to life in Australia was to learn a new language: Cantonese. 'It was the only way to communicate with the people who worked in the restaurant in Perth,' he says in Cantonese without a trace of an accent.

While Tom was born in Vietnam, his family is actually Chinese. In the 1910s, his grandfather (then eighteen years old) moved to Vietnam from Chaozhou (sometimes written as Teochew), a province in Guangdong (also known as Canton), which is in the south of China. He grew up in a family where the men prepared the food for special occasions, like Lunar New Year and weddings. These days, diners from Perth call the day before they arrive to ask Tom to prepare classic Chaozhou dishes, such as fried tofu prawns, and soy sauce-braised duck.

The most popular items on the regular menu are Singapore noodles, char kway teow, satay, honey chicken, and black bean beef, although Tom has noticed a new trend. These days, there are more people ordering vegetables. 'Most tables will order a plate of vegetables to go with their dishes,' says Tom. He's also noticed that things are very different from when he first learned to cook. 'Back then, we boiled chicken and then shredded the meat to cook with. If you did that now, no one would eat it.'

From not wanting to be a chef, Tom has turned into someone who likes to watch YouTube videos of Chinese chefs in order to learn new techniques, like roasting barbecue meats. 'I like to think that every day I can get better as a chef. If you believe there's a ceiling then you can't improve anymore. And I don't want to stop learning.'

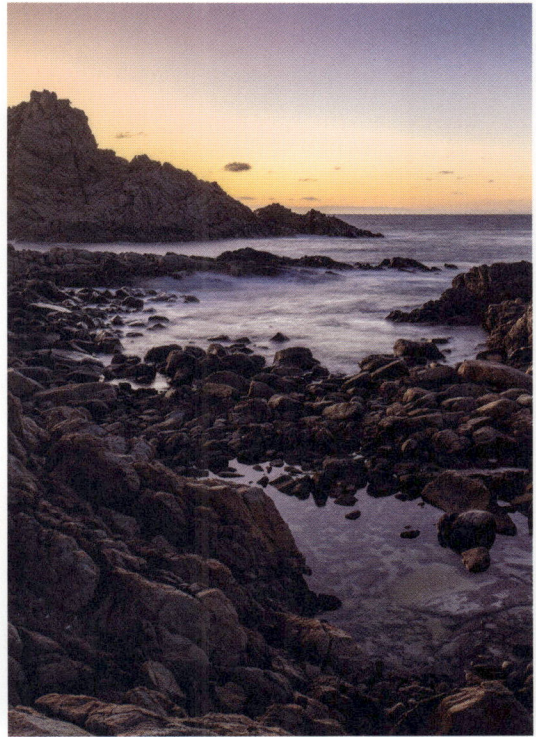

Tom applies this same devotion to his bonsai. He was in his forties when he started to pay attention to the trees he was seeing on his weekly drives from Australind to Perth to buy stock for the restaurant. 'I wondered what it would take to make a tree very small,' he says. 'So I started to read lots of books about bonsai. And I realised that cooking and bonsai are similar because they both require patience.'

'To make a dish good, you have to put in a lot of effort. You have to give it your all – what ingredients go in? How do I make the presentation look good? It's the same with bonsai. You have to give it so much careful and constant attention,' says Tom.

Tom's now sixty-eight. His plan is to work for two or three more years and then retire, so he can spend more time with his family and his plants.

SESAME PRAWN TOAST

Sesame prawn toast is a classic way to begin any Australian Chinese meal, hailing from a Hong Kong tradition of Western-style afternoon tea snacks. There's no reason why this happy marriage of prawns and white bread can't be a regular feature in your home. The trick to making prawn toast is to use frozen bread, not fresh bread, so that the toast maintains its shape.

MAKES 20

20 raw prawns (about 240 g), shelled and deveined with tails removed

1 teaspoon salt

1 teaspoon sugar

1 teaspoon white pepper

a few drops of sesame oil

1 egg, lightly beaten

vegetable or canola oil, for deep-frying

4 slices frozen white bread

100 g sesame seeds

Sweet and sour sauce, to serve (see page 129 to make your own, or use store-bought)

Use a cleaver to smash each prawn, and then finely chop until a paste-like consistency. If you do not have a cleaver, use a blender to blend the prawns into a paste-like consistency.

Combine prawns, salt, sugar, pepper, sesame oil and egg in a bowl and mix well.

Fill a large wok or saucepan approximately two-thirds full with oil. Slowly bring to 180°C over medium–high heat. This might take up to 10 minutes.

Spoon a quarter of the prawn mixture onto 1 slice of bread and use a butter knife to spread it smoothly and evenly right to the crusts. Repeat with remaining prawn mixture and bread. Cut each slice in half diagonally to create 2 triangles.

Place sesame seeds in a small plate or shallow bowl. Place prawn-covered bread, prawn side down, onto sesame seeds. Dip the cut edge of the bread into the sesame seeds.

Once the oil is hot, fry the triangles of bread in the oil, prawn side down, until golden, flipping occasionally. Serve with sweet and sour sauce.

FIVE SPICE SALT CHILLI PORK CHOPS

Five spice powder is a common Cantonese ingredient made with cinnamon, cloves, fennel seeds, Sichuan peppercorn, and star anise. It adds an energising fragrance to every dish it's used in, from roast duck to these pork chops. The fragrance just keeps on building as you make this dish: first with the garlic, spring onions, and five spice, and finally with that hit of shaoxing wine. The salt and pepper mix in this recipe also goes well with tofu – make extra and keep it in an airtight jar for sprinkling onto other dishes. It will last for six months, although you will probably eat it all before then.

4 pork loin chops
1 tablespoon shaoxing rice wine
2 teaspoons salt
1 teaspoon sugar
4 tablespoons cornflour
3 tablespoons water
vegetable or canola oil, for deep-frying
2 tablespoons vegetable oil, extra, for stir-frying
4 garlic cloves, finely chopped
2 spring onions, finely chopped
2 tablespoons fried shallots
1 long red chilli, chopped
chilli crisp oil, to taste, optional
a dash of shaoxing rice wine, extra

SALT AND PEPPER MIX

2 teaspoons salt
1 teaspoon white pepper
½ teaspoon sugar
½ teaspoon five spice powder
½ teaspoon MSG, optional

Cut each pork chop into four pieces. (Using a cleaver means that you'll be able to chop through the bones with ease. If you have a regular knife that does not cut through bone, remove the bones first.)

Combine pork with shaoxing wine, salt, and sugar in a large bowl. Mix well to combine, and refrigerate, covered, for at least 30 minutes.

Add 2 tablespoons of cornflour to the pork mixture and mix well so that the pork is covered evenly. Add water and mix well, then add the remaining cornflour so that a light batter forms around the pork.

To make the salt and pepper mix, combine the mix ingredients in a small bowl.

Fill a large wok or saucepan approximately two-thirds full with oil. Slowly bring to 180°C over medium–high heat. This might take up to 10 minutes. Once the oil is hot, fry the pork in batches until golden, stirring frequently so that the pieces don't stick to each other and can cook evenly. Remove from the oil. Then add it back into the hot oil and fry again until golden. Remove the pork from the oil and place on a colander or wire rack to drain and cool.

In the wok, heat the extra vegetable oil. Add the garlic. Once it's fragrant, add the spring onions, fried shallots, long red chilli, and chilli crisp oil, if using. Stir-fry until fragrant. Add the pork and stir-fry until mixed well.

Sprinkle the salt and pepper mix on top and stir-fry until the salt and pepper is evenly spread. Add a dash of extra shaoxing wine and stir-fry to mix well.

SATAY VEGETABLES

While satay is Indonesian in origin, the satay sauce that Tom cooks with at Dunsborough Chinese is a house mix that uses Jimmy's Saté Sauce – a Hong Kong favourite – as a base, to which he adds coconut milk, a peanut sauce, and other secret ingredients. For the convenience of cooking at home, Tom recommends using Jimmy's Saté Sauce or finding your own favourite brand of satay sauce.

300 g of mixed vegetables,
   for example:
      100 g broccoli, cut into florets
      100 g cauliflower, cut into florets
      50 g carrots, cut into sticks
      50 g baby corn, roughly chopped
      ½ small onion, sliced
2 tablespoons vegetable oil
100 ml chicken or vegetable stock
6 tablespoons Jimmy's Saté Sauce

Cover vegetables in boiling water for 2 minutes and drain.

Heat the oil in a wok or large pan on high heat. Add the vegetables and stir-fry for a few minutes.

Add the stock. Bring to the boil then reduce heat and simmer until vegetables are cooked.

Add the satay sauce and mix well to combine.

A HANDY GUIDE TO CHOPSTICKS ETIQUETTE

When you use chopsticks, you're instantly connected with 5000 years of Chinese culture, according to cultural consultant Lydia Feng. Here are eight do's and don'ts to ensure you're not being rude or waking up the ancestors when you use chopsticks:

1 To avoid being rude, don't use your chopsticks to point at people or things.

2 If communal chopsticks are available, use those to bring the food to your bowl (or plate), and then use your own chopsticks to eat. If they're not available and you're using your own chopsticks, always bring the food from the plate to your own bowl (or plate) before eating. Don't pick up the food with your chopsticks and bring it directly to your mouth. That's also rude.

3 Don't suck on the ends of the chopsticks (even if the sauce is delicious). Again, considered rude.

4 Keep your chopsticks level. Don't hold them with one sticking up above the other; it's associated with death. The reason? 'In China, you only use unlevel wood to make coffins,' says Lydia.

5 Never stick your chopsticks upright in your bowl of rice. It looks like incense sticks, which are used to pay respects to the dead. To rest your chopsticks, place them horizontally on your bowl or plate.

6 Don't use your chopsticks to rummage in a dish. 'In Chinese there's a saying, "Don't use your chopsticks like they're lost children wandering around",' says Lydia. Instead, reach directly for the piece of food closest to you, and only touch what you intend to pick up and eat.

7 Don't use your chopsticks like drumsticks to tap on bowls or plates. The action is associated with begging.

8 Finally, don't drop your chopsticks. 'If you drop your chopsticks, you may upset the dead ancestors of the place where you're eating,' says Lydia.

福

A FISH OUT OF WATER

PAGODA CHINESE RESTAURANT

ATHERTON, QUEENSLAND

When it comes to Chinese restaurants with the best views, the Pagoda in Atherton is up there; its panoramic windows face the mountains, creating a skyline that wouldn't be out of place in a Chinese ink painting.

Atherton is in far north Queensland, about a ninety minute drive south-west of Cairns. It's in the lush and fertile Tablelands region, which grows coffee, peanuts, mangoes, and pineapples. Atherton is home to 7000 people, including Tina Tan and Andy Liu who run the Pagoda, and their three kids.

Tina and Andy immigrated to Australia in 2013 from Guangzhou, the capital of Guangdong (Canton) province in south China, where they were fish farmers. The business environment there wasn't ideal, says Andy, which was why he was happy that his sister in Australia could sponsor their family to come over. When Andy first arrived, he spent some time working at her Chinese restaurant in Mackay. 'Simply looking at my shape, you'll know that my career is about food,' he jokes. Not long after, he learned that the thirty-year-old Pagoda restaurant was for sale. So he and Tina drove the eight hours to check it out … and never looked back.

Adapting to life in Atherton was tough at first. 'Most of our staff were Australians and it was difficult to communicate. I only knew three English phrases: "Thank you. How are you? Bye-bye."' says Tina.

'Many people know us as there are only a few Chinese here. When we go out, people know we're the owners of Pagoda. Like on Monday, when I went out to buy coffee, the barista recognised me and said that I live opposite his house. But I didn't recognise him as most Australians look alike to me,' says Tina.

There was also the issue of the food being so different to the Chinese food they were used to in Guangzhou. 'When I made Australian Chinese food for the first time, I found it very easy to do,' says Andy. 'But it wasn't the same taste for new Chinese migrants like us. The taste was totally different; it was much sweeter.'

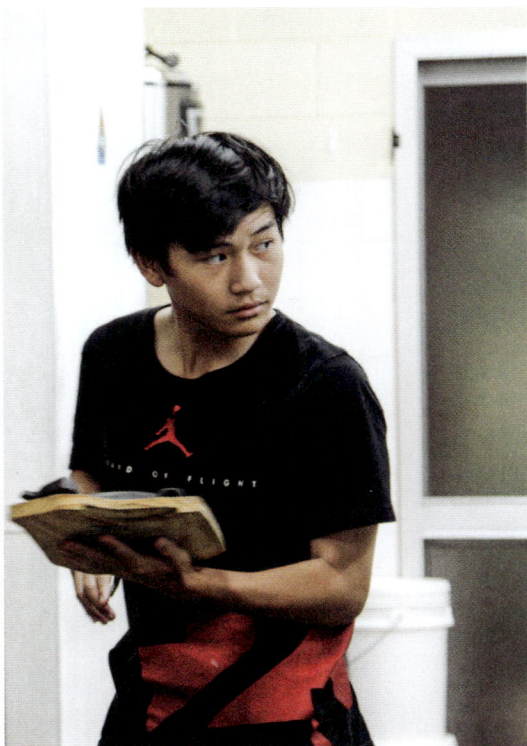

Over the years, Tina and Andy have experimented with serving dishes they know from Guangzhou, like salted egg yolk prawns. 'But the locals prefer our popular dishes, like deep-fried duck with chilli plum sauce,' says Tina.

A much-loved offering at the Pagoda is their $37 four-course banquet menu, which starts with either chicken sweet corn soup or crab meat sweet corn soup. The entree is deep-fried mixed seafood with prawn chips, which is followed by fried rice and a choice of eight mains, such as sizzling garlic prawns, salt and pepper squid, or the deep-fried duck with chilli plum sauce, just to name a few. For dessert (if you still have room), with your tea or coffee you can have lychees with ice cream or deep-fried ice cream. It comes cheerfully topped with a colourful paper umbrella, like a tropical cocktail.

Tina and Andy's kids all adapted quickly to the new, sweet tastes of Australian Chinese food. The restaurant lifestyle, however, was a different matter. 'When parents run a restaurant, it's common for the kids to get involved and help,' says Tina. 'When our eldest son was in year six, he'd ask why his classmates didn't need to work but he had to.'

'Sometimes we tease our kids and ask them if they want to be a chef like their dad. Our younger son doesn't say yes or no, he just says, "I don't know".'

Atherton is no stranger to Chinese settlement. At one point in the early 1890s, there were more than 1000 Chinese people living here, enough for a bustling Chinatown with its very own pig oven. They'd first arrived in the 1880s when the Tablelands opened up for timber cutting and growing maize. 'The Chinese were very good at that,' says local historian Gordon Grimwade. But the population eventually left Atherton. 'After the First World War, a lot of returned service people were allocated farm leases at the expense of the Chinese who were already leasing that land,' says Gordon. 'It tended to break down the structure of the Chinese economy.'

Today, there are still signs of the early Chinese presence in Atherton. The Hou Wang Temple is the oldest original-standing Chinese temple of its type in Australia. It was completed in 1903, damaged by a cyclone in 1950, and rebuilt in 1988. The temple worships a military general from the Song Dynasty. Much of the exquisite timber work was made by expert artisans in Guangzhou and shipped to Australia.

At Pagoda, the preservation of Chinese culture continues in other ways. Every year, the restaurant hosts visiting schools from Cairns who bring their students for a Chinese meal, which they get to eat with chopsticks. The chopsticks are a popular hit with the locals.

'We ordered a lot of special chopsticks from China, and some of them are gold-plated,' says Tina. 'But the chopsticks go missing from time to time. Many of our customers asked if they could take them home. That's fine with us. It's easy for us to order these chopsticks. We're glad that they're so interested in them.'

SWEET AND SOUR PORK

It's hard to imagine Australian Chinese cuisine without sweet and sour pork, with its bright red sauce and chunks of pineapple. This is a dish with origins that can be traced back to a menu written in the Tang Dynasty, in 708AD. The addition of ketchup as a sweetener is one example of how the dish has evolved to suit the Western palate. To achieve the cheerful red colour of the sauce, Andy from Pagoda adds a roll of haw flakes, a small, thin, chewy snack made with hawthorn berries. Haw flakes are available at Asian supermarkets, and also in the memories of children who grew up with them in their pockets, ready to snack on at a moment's notice.

vegetable or canola oil,
   for deep-frying
150g pineapple pieces, canned
   or fresh (if fresh needs to be
   very ripe and sweet)
½ red capsicum, chopped
½ green capsicum, chopped
½ onion, chopped
½ carrot, sliced

MARINATED PORK

350 g pork neck
1 teaspoon salt
1 teaspoon sugar
⅛ teaspoon MSG
¼ teaspoon white pepper
½ egg white
1 tablespoon cornflour

BATTER

20 g cornflour
60 g self-raising flour
100 ml water
1 tablespoon cornflour, extra

To make the marinated pork, slice the pork neck into long strips and then cut into 1.5 cm cubes. Rinse the pork thoroughly under cold running water and then drain. In a bowl, combine the pork, salt, sugar, MSG and pepper. Mix well.

Add the egg white, stir to combine and then finally add the cornflour. Mix well again. Refrigerate pork mixture for 20 minutes.

To make the batter, combine the cornflour, self-raising flour and water in a medium bowl.

Remove the pork mixture from the fridge, add the extra tablespoon of cornflour and mix well. Add the batter mixture to the pork mixture and mix well.

Fill a deep saucepan or wok approximately two-thirds full with oil. Slowly bring to 150°C over medium–high heat. This might take up to 10 minutes. Drop each piece of pork individually into the oil to make sure they don't clump together.

SWEET AND SOUR SAUCE

200 ml water

3 tablespoons white sugar

3 tablespoons tomato sauce

3 tablespoons white vinegar

1 tablespoon cornflour

1 roll of haw flakes, optional

Deep-fry pork in batches until golden and cooked through. Drain on a plate lined with paper towel.

To make the sweet and sour sauce, place the sweet and sour sauce ingredients in a wok on high heat and bring to the boil.

Add the pineapple and vegetables. Simmer for 1 minute, then add the pork. Toss quickly until pork is well coated in the sauce. Serve immediately.

BRAISED KING PRAWNS WITH GARLIC SAUCE

Fresh, fragrant, and simple to make at home, this dish is sure to be a new weeknight favourite. It's a Hong Kong restaurant-style dish that you can unlock the secret to with one simple trick: fry half the garlic until it's golden brown, then save it for sprinkling back into your finished dish of prawns cooked in garlic oil. It's your golden ticket to garlicky goodness.

250 g chopped mixed vegetables, for example: broccoli, cauliflower, carrots, baby corn

3 tablespoons vegetable oil

10 garlic cloves, roughly chopped

16–20 large raw prawns, shelled and deveined with tails intact

100 ml chicken stock

2 teaspoons sugar

2 tablespoons cornflour

Cover the vegetables in boiling water, then immediately rinse them in cold water.

In a wok or large pan, heat the vegetable oil and add half the garlic. Stir-fry until fragrant. When the garlic is golden, remove it from the wok or pan and transfer to a small bowl. Leave most of the oil in the wok or pan.

Add the remaining garlic to the wok or pan and stir-fry until fragrant. Then add the prawns and stir-fry until they're almost cooked.

Add the vegetables, chicken stock, and sugar. Stir-fry to combine and bring to the boil. Simmer for about 2 minutes. Add the cornflour and stir-fry to mix well. Add the reserved garlic and stir-fry until mixed in with the prawns and vegetables.

DEEP-FRIED DUCK WITH CHILLI PLUM SAUCE

It's easy to understand why this dish, a play on the traditional roast duck with plum sauce, is one of the best-selling dishes at Pagoda. No Cantonese barbecue meats shop would be complete without a window full of glistening roast ducks, which are served with plum sauce for dipping. Pagoda adds a chilli kick to the plum sauce, which lovingly coats the duck with a mild sweet and sour heat. Serve with fried rice or white rice to soak up the bright red sauce (that you'll be wanting to put on everything).

vegetable or canola oil, for deep-frying
½ whole duck, deboned
plain flour, for coating the duck

BATTER

20 g cornflour
60 g self-raising flour
100 ml water
1 tablespoon cornflour

CHILLI PLUM SAUCE

3 garlic cloves, finely chopped
6 tablespoons Sweet and sour sauce (see page 129 to make your own, or use store-bought)
6 tablespoons plum sauce
6 tablespoons tomato sauce
2 tablespoons chilli sauce (or to taste)
1 teaspoon sugar, optional
1 tablespoon cornflour, optional

Fill a wok or large pan approximately two-thirds full with oil. Slowly bring to 60–70°C over medium–high heat. This might take up to 10 minutes.

To make the batter, combine all batter ingredients in a large bowl and stir to mix well.

Lightly coat the duck with plain flour, and then coat the duck in batter.

Lower the duck gently into the hot oil. Using tongs or a slotted spoon, move it around the oil and flip it over occasionally so it cooks evenly. To avoid the duck burning, turn down the heat when the duck begins to turn golden, around 3 minutes. Keep the duck turning in the oil until it is golden, then remove from heat and drain on a colander or wire rack.

To make the chilli plum sauce, cook the garlic in a wok or large pan until fragrant. Then add the sweet and sour sauce, plum sauce, tomato sauce, and chilli sauce. Stir for a few minutes or until the sauce starts to thicken and come to the boil. If the sauce is not sweet enough, add a teaspoon of sugar. If the sauce is too thin, add a tablespoon of cornflour and stir well. Remove from heat.

Slice the duck into pieces about 2 cm-wide, and serve with sauce ladled over.

THE STORY OF THE
LAZY SUSAN

It's hard to imagine a Chinese restaurant without a Lazy Susan, this wonder of a spinning turntable. How else are we supposed to shorten the distance between ourselves and the fried rice? Rise up from our vinyl chairs and lean across the table? Ask the person next to you to pass the plate?

Thanks to the Lazy Susan, we can stay seated from the moment the prawn crackers hit the table to the final spoonful of deep-fried ice cream, with no need to ask our table buddies to pass anything our way, but who do we have to thank for this mechanical marvel?

Who invented it? Who was Susan? And just how lazy was she?

CIRCLING BACK TO THE BEGINNING

If we go way back in time, the Chinese dined on square or rectangular tables, so the history of the Lazy Susan actually doesn't begin in China.

Some people would have you believe that the Lazy Susan was invented by American Founding Father Thomas Jefferson, the third President of the United States, and the author of the Declaration of Independence (or perhaps the Declaration of Independently Moving Food Close to You). The myth goes that he invented the device to serve his daughter, Susan (who was presumably quite lazy?) – except that even though Jefferson fathered numerous children, none of them were called Susan.

The Lazy Susan's origin story actually begins in France some time in the middle of the eighteenth century. It was a wheeled serving tray called an étagère, and became a common serving device to replace the duties of maids and footmen. Later, the étagère was introduced to England, where

it was known as a dumbwaiter, thus beginning the tradition of giving this handy turntable quite insulting names.

A hundred years later, this device evolved to become round tables which could be multi-tiered – all the better to spin drinks and snacks around for your guests to access with ease.

Amidst all this spinning and drinking and snacking, someone had the bright idea to put a spinning table on top of a normal table. In 1891, Elizabeth Howell of Missouri filed a patent for this idea, which was, one could say, revolutionary. Elizabeth Howell's self-waiting table had a movable portion, which was supported by rollers and mounted on a central pivot, and completely turned the tables on the idea that food had to stay in one location.

THE ASIAN CONNECTION

In 1915, Malaysian doctor, Wu Lian De, had a similar idea for a moving table, but for very different reasons. Dr Wu believed that communal Chinese meals were a hotbed of potential contagion for conditions such as pneumonia and tuberculosis. Tuberculosis is actually not transmitted by saliva, but Dr Wu wasn't to know that when he came up with the idea of putting a revolving tray on a table. On the tray would be dishes for sharing, but now each dish would have its own spoon so that diners could scoop food into their bowls, instead of dipping their chopsticks into dishes.

Unfortunately, there's no evidence that Dr Wu's proposal to use moving tables caught on in China or South-East Asia at the time, even though these days serving spoons and communal chopsticks are as common on the table as plates and bowls.

LAZY SUSAN COMES AROUND

The first verified mention of the 'Lazy Susan' can be found in *Vanity Fair* magazine in 1917, where a revolving server was advertised under this name for the grand price of $8.50.

In the mid-1950s, Chinese restaurants were flourishing in the United States. George Hall, a friend of one of the restaurateurs, toyed with some ball bearings and a round piece of wood, creating a version of the Lazy Susan as we know it today.

By 1972, when US President Richard Nixon famously dined with Chinese Premier Zhou En Lai during his visit to China, the Lazy Susan was front and centre, basking in the glow of chopstick diplomacy.

These days, the Lazy Susan is so popular in Chinese restaurants around the world that it's literally part of the furniture. It's hard to imagine a banquet-ful of dishes without one. In China, some Lazy Susans are even automated to spin constantly throughout the meal. So while we still have no idea who Susan is, perhaps we can all agree: if Susan is the turntable, there's definitely nothing lazy about her.

WHEN LIFE GIVES YOU LEMON CHICKEN

GAWLER PALACE

GAWLER, SOUTH AUSTRALIA

Lemon chicken is one of the most popular dishes at Gawler Palace. Vinh Chiem, who's Vietnamese and runs the restaurant with his family, has tried to understand this curiosity.

'When I look at lemon chicken, it's so monotonous in colour. I don't even think it's worthy of putting on Instagram,' he says, bemused. 'But the amount we sell is phenomenal. I would put it down to just extreme flavours: salty chicken, and really sweet and tangy lemon sauce.'

Gawler Palace is in the heart of Gawler, the oldest country town in South Australia, forty kilometres north of Adelaide and on the road to the vineyards of the Barossa Valley. It's a long, deep restaurant made festive by Christmas lights that stay up long after December, making it perfect for the hundreds of thousands of local birthdays, anniversaries, and celebrations of lemon chicken that they've hosted since 1985.

The restaurant is run by Vinh, his parents, Kim Chiem and Thanh Ho, and his brother Phuong. Kim and Thanh took over Gawler Palace after running a Vietnamese restaurant and working in market gardens around Adelaide. They came to Australia from Vietnam as refugees via Malaysia in 1977, and met on the boat that Thanh drove from Malaysia to Darwin. The journey took three weeks.

When Thanh first arrived in Australia, he worked in Chinese restaurants for two years. 'Before, Vietnamese restaurants were not really busy,' says Thanh, 'but Chinese restaurants did very well.'

The chefs in the kitchen were not keen to teach Thanh too much, for fear that he would take his newfound knowledge and go elsewhere to work. It was the previous owner of Gawler Palace who taught Thanh how to make all the sauces he uses today – lemon sauce, honey sauce, Mongolian sauce.

While Vietnamese food is very popular now, Vinh and his family have stuck to serving Australian Chinese classics. 'We've dabbled in Vietnamese food, but the problem is because we're called Gawler Palace Chinese Restaurant, most people don't expect to see Vietnamese food here,' says Vinh.

'The dish that's closest to having any kind of Vietnamese influence is the lemongrass chicken or beef. It's something that we have at home. Dad said, "We've got to have it on the menu",' says Vinh. 'It's a bit of our roots.'

At Gawler Palace, diners are greeted by Kim, who runs the front of house. Thanh is head chef, Phuong is sous chef, and Vinh manages the restaurant. His day starts with showing up at 6 am to tend to the house stock ('It's a chicken stock six hours in the making and it's almost like a bone broth by the end.') and ends at 9 or 10 pm after he's checked inventory levels and packed all the food back into the cool room.

Regulars have watched Vinh and Phuong grow up over the years; some have been going to the restaurant for more than three decades. One of the more recent regulars is local winemaker Tina Kies. 'We've been going there every Thursday night for ten years, basically since the kids left home,' she says.

Over the years, Tina has helped Vinh come up with a list of wines that pair well with the dishes at Gawler Palace, such as rosés, which Tina believes go best with sweet and sour pork. 'You don't want anything too overbearing with a sweet and sour pork, so look for something that's fairly light and soft.'

With black bean beef, Tina recommends a Barossa Klauber Block Shiraz. 'Pairing beef with something red is great', she says. The ever popular lemon chicken, meanwhile, would go well with a fruit-driven riesling. 'I would probably go with the beautiful Barossa riesling,' says Tina.

And finally, with deep-fried ice cream, Tina suggests the Heysen Gold Frontignac, a sweet white wine. 'It's like a white frontignac, almost moscato-style,' she says. 'Or you could always go with the tawny port, which is fantastic as well.'

She draws on a German wine lineage that goes all the way back to the 1800s. 'My husband's family were vignerons and came from Germany in 1867,' says Tina. 'They came out here because of religious persecution, and ended up in the Barossa Valley.' Tina's father-in-law started making wine in 1969, and Kies Family Wines have been making wine ever since.

Tina's not the only local to be part of the Gawler Palace story, with many young people employed there over the years, doing everything from prepping ingredients to looking after the customers. 'Right now I've got a high school student working the woks,' says Vinh. 'She just picked it up so quickly, and we'll miss her when she goes on her gap year.'

Before Covid, Gawler Palace was a popular place for Chinese tourists on bus tours to the Barossa. 'They'd be a bit bamboozled by some of the selection, which is often deep-fried, battered, and very sweet,' says Vinh.

'One of the things I do remember is when they ordered the soup, and we had one little bowl come out, they were like, "Where's the rest of it?" In Chinese culture, when they order a soup, they get a big bowl in the middle, and they will share it. The look on that person's face when it came out was like, "Is that it?"'

For Kim, connecting with diners has been one of the most important and rewarding things about running the restaurant. 'We look after customers. They're very happy, and they come back,' says Kim. 'They enjoy it and we enjoy it. It's very friendly, like family.'

And like all families, there's acceptance...even though you may not understand entirely why they have such love for lemon chicken.

LEMON CHICKEN

While many people think that lemon chicken must surely be a local invention, it's actually been served in Hong Kong since the 1960s. This tangy dish is still available today in Hong Kong's old-school diners, served with rice, or even pasta. Gawler Palace's version is renowned for being particularly crispy and tangy. The crispiness of the chicken comes from frying it twice, and the extreme lemon flavour comes from three sources of lemon goodness. So now when life gives you lemons, make lemon chicken.

1 chicken breast, cut into 1 cm-thick slices
½ teaspoon salt
½ teaspoon MSG
white pepper, to taste
a few drops of sesame oil
2 tablespoons cornflour, for coating
vegetable or canola oil, for deep-frying
sesame seeds, to garnish
lemon wedges, to serve

BATTER

1 cup cornflour
¼ cup self-raising flour

LEMON SAUCE

¼ cup lemon juice
¼ cup sugar
⅔ cup water
5 tablespoons white vinegar
1 teaspoon salt
3 fresh celery leaves
2 tablespoons lemon essence
⅓ cup lemon cordial
yellow food colouring, optional

CORNFLOUR SLURRY

1 tablespoon cornflour mixed with 1 tablespoon water

In a large bowl, combine chicken with salt, MSG, pepper and a few drops of sesame oil. Cover and refrigerate for 30 minutes.

To make the batter, in a bowl, combine cornflour and self-raising flour, then slowly add water until consistency coats the back of a spoon.

Lightly coat the chicken in cornflour, shake off any excess, and then dip it into the batter.

Fill a large wok or saucepan approximately two-thirds full with oil. Slowly bring to 180°C over medium–high heat. This might take up to 10 minutes. Fry the chicken until it takes on a hint of colour. Remove and set aside to cool and drain. Continue to heat the oil until it reaches 200°C and then return the chicken and fry until it is golden.

Remove the chicken from the oil and drain on a wire rack.

To make the lemon sauce, combine the lemon sauce ingredients in a small saucepan and bring to the boil. Remove from heat. Remove and discard celery leaves.

Add cornflour slurry to the lemon sauce and mix to thicken.

To serve, chop the chicken into 3 cm-wide pieces and top with lemon sauce. Sprinkle with sesame seeds and serve with lemon wedges.

CRISPY STEAK IN PLUM SAUCE

Two types of plum sauce join forces here to create a crispy steak that you'll keep coming back to for more. If you're a huge sweet and sour fan and looking for something with more complex sour flavours, this is definitely the dish for you. This dish is also known as Peking shredded beef on some menus, and is appreciated for its bold flavours. If ordering this dish at a restaurant, one might also order a bok choy with mushrooms to balance out the flavours.

200g topside beef, sliced into strips as thinly as possible, ideally 5 mm thick

400g cornflour

vegetable or canola oil, for deep-frying

toasted sesame seeds, to garnish

crispy rice noodles, to serve

PLUM SAUCE

¼ cup Pun Chun Plum Sauce

¼ cup Lee Kum Kee Plum Sauce

3 tablespoons vinegar

3 tablespoons ketchup

1 tablespoon Worcestershire sauce

1 teaspoon salt

¼ cup sugar

½ cup water

CORNFLOUR SLURRY

1 tablespoon cornflour mixed with 1 tablespoon water

Coat the beef strips in cornflour.

Fill a wok or large frying pan approximately two-thirds full with oil. Slowly bring to 200°C over medium–high heat. This might take up to 10 minutes. Fry the beef for 30 seconds. Remove and drain and cool in a colander. Continue to heat the oil until it reaches 200°C and fry the beef again for 30 seconds. Drain and cool again. Reheat the oil to 200°C and then fry the beef again.

To make the plum sauce, combine all the ingredients in a saucepan. Bring to the boil, then remove from heat. Add cornflour slurry and mix to thicken.

Drain the oil used for deep-frying and heat the wok again over medium heat. Add the crispy beef and desired amount of sauce. Toss to evenly coat the beef. Serve garnished with toasted sesame seeds on a bed of crispy rice noodles, if using.

CHICKEN AND SWEET CORN SOUP

In the early twentieth century, China and Hong Kong began importing canned fruit and canned corn from America. Canned items were seen as luxury items, and it's believed that chicken and corn soup originated in China and Hong Kong before it made its way to America and Australia where it became a popular starter. Tucking into a bowl of chicken and sweet corn soup is one of the cosiest ways to begin a meal. It's perfect for rainy day comfort eating, too, and so simple to whip up. You'll always have creamed corn and sweet corn in the pantry after making this for the first time.

½ teaspoon salt, plus extra to season
1 teaspoon MSG
a few drops of sesame oil
1 chicken breast
2 cups chicken stock
1 × 420 g can creamed corn
1 × 420 g can sweet corn, drained
dried parsley leaves or chopped fresh chives, to garnish

POTATO STARCH SLURRY
1 tablespoon potato starch mixed with 1 tablespoon water

Combine salt, half the MSG and sesame oil in a medium bowl. Add chicken and refrigerate, covered, for at least 2 hours.

Bring water to the boil in a small pot. Add chicken and simmer until the internal temperature of the chicken reaches 80°C. Once the chicken is cooked, place in a bowl of iced water to stop it cooking further.

When the chicken is cool, dice it into 1 cm cubes.

In a large pot or saucepan, bring chicken stock and the creamed corn to the boil. Just before it boils, add the slurry to thicken soup to your desired consistency. Season with remaining MSG and extra salt.

To serve, place diced chicken and one tablespoon of canned sweet corn into each serving bowl, and fill with soup. Garnish with dried parsley leaves or chopped fresh chives.

CHINESE RESTAURANTS AS TIME TRAVEL

Vintage Chinese restaurants appeal to me and Josh because we love places that exude character and history. We've been to one hundred of them around the country, and there's still many more to visit! The colourful theatricality transports you to another time and place. I love how the decor in Chinese restaurants gives diners something to occupy their minds while they are waiting for their food. Growing up in a small coastal town north of Sydney, a trip to the local Chinese restaurant offered an escape from monoculture. It was 1987, *The Australian Women's Weekly* cookbooks reigned supreme, and taking a spin on the Lazy Susan was as close as I was getting to experiencing other cultures.

Our quest is to document these restaurants on Instagram with our account @ChineseRestaurantRoadtrip before they are modernised or gone forever. And what a great excuse to hit the road and venture to places you've never been before! Classic Chinese restaurants in Australia evoke a lot of memories for people and we tap into that by styling me for the photos. The very nature of each restaurant inspires my various sartorial escapades. I dress up in vintage clothing that responds to the style and decor – a largely intuitive process that has been known to lead me down internet wormholes late at night!

We look for unique time capsules mainly from the 1960s–80s with original decor and signage. The ones we choose have noteworthy

aesthetics that provide clues into the mysteries of the past and take you on an armchair holiday.

Ho's Palace in Blackheath was one of the first Chinese restaurants we took photos of. I love the ornate setting with colour symbolism found in temple interiors in China. This photo (below) is of me on my birthday in fairly '80s getup, tucking into a slice of birthday cake, which I think is really true to people's experience of going out for Chinese to celebrate important milestones.

On these trips, Josh and I typically order the special fried rice. It's a mainstay that's always on the menu and is usually indicative of the overall quality of the food. Honey prawns are another favourite – such a fun dish that doesn't take itself too seriously!

Here (above) you can see Chan's Canton Village, which is in Casula on the outskirts of south-west suburban Sydney, and was established in 1979. As you arrive at the entrance of the car park you are greeted by a grand archway (paifang) with a classic green pagoda roof. In the 1970s, with the arrival of entrepreneurial Hong Kongers and Cantonese migrants, Chinese restaurant design in Australia became more upmarket and Chan's perfectly embodies that era.

The ambiance is unique at every turn. The interior is really ornate and the design throughout echoes Chinese temples, palaces, and gardens. The ceiling motif design references the Forbidden Palace, for instance. Once inside, there's a moon gate like you'd find in a Chinese garden, and red and gold Axminster carpet shimmers underfoot. The '80s dream is alive and well in there. They even have a bar where the waiter shook me up a mint green grasshopper cocktail to accompany my prawn crackers before the entrees arrived! Truly glorious Aussie Chinese restaurant heaven.

**WORDS BY ANNA SATIN
AND PHOTOS BY JOSHUA BURNS**

FROM PADDOCK TO PLATE

T'S CHINESE RESTAURANT

SHEFFIELD, TASMANIA

Alex Zhao was working the woks one night when his neighbour rang to say that one of Alex's cows had escaped and was heading down the road. When you're both the paddock *and* the plate in T's Paddock to Plate Chinese restaurant, sometimes mid-stir-fry you just have to jump on your motorcycle and go retrieve a cow.

T's is the only Chinese restaurant in Sheffield, a town of around 1600 people in the north of Tasmania, which is a popular destination for people on their way to Cradle Mountain. It sits on the main street near a bakehouse and a pizzeria, with a view of Mount Roland, a majestic rocky range which stands 1233 metres above sea level.

The restaurant, which is also the only paddock to plate Chinese restaurant in Australia, is named after Tamara, Alex's grandmother on his mother's side. Alex's parents are from Urumqi, the capital of Xinjiang in north-west China. His dad Victor is Chinese, and his mum Sonya is half Chinese and half Russian. They left Urumqi as refugees in 1985, stopping for two months in Hong Kong where Alex was born, before arriving in Sydney.

They stayed there for eleven years – it's where Alex's two younger sisters were born – and looked for a farm where they could settle. Growing up in the city of Urumqi, it was Victor's dream to be a farmer. Eventually, in 2000, they settled in Sheffield because it was affordable. 'We were the first Chinese family to move to the district,' says Alex, 'and we felt very welcome.'

The family farm, which Alex runs, is an 80-hectare property with 200 Dorper sheep, 40 Berkshire pigs, and 40 Angus lowline cows. Alex also runs T's with his wife Sammi – she's front of house, Alex is in the kitchen with Victor, Sonya helps out when it gets very busy, and an Italian-named robot, Bella, brings out the dishes. 'It's very multicultural,' quips Sammi.

Northern Chinese cuisine features proudly on the T's menu, where cumin-spiced lamb from Dorper sheep is used for hand-pulled noodles, and pork from Berkshire pigs is stuffed in pan-fried potstickers. Angus beef is served as beef and black bean in a nod to traditional Australian Chinese cooking, and the black bean sauce is made from scratch. Even the chilli crisp oil is homemade using Xinjiang chillies grown and dried on the family farm. If the weather's been kind that season, the Chinese broccoli, carrots, and zucchini in stir-fries are homegrown too.

In 2013, T's was listed in the annual Phaidon book, *Where Chefs Eat*, where Anthony Lui (executive chef and co-owner of Flower Drum, the esteemed Melbourne Chinese restaurant), praised their lamb and dumplings and described T's as a 'humble restaurant doing spectacular food'. But there was a time before T's became destination dining.

When the family arrived in Sheffield in 2000, they had no farming experience. They began with cattle, and it did not go well. 'Whenever a cow got sick, we didn't know what was going on,' says Alex. 'So we'd run over to the neighbours and they'd help us out.' Their dream of being self-sufficient on the farm did not work out, and several years later they were in debt. Then an opportunity came up to buy the oldest building in town, which came with a homemade ice cream business. Alex and his sisters Katrisha and Karina ran the shop after school. The first time they made $100, they were so excited that they closed the shop and ran home to tell their parents.

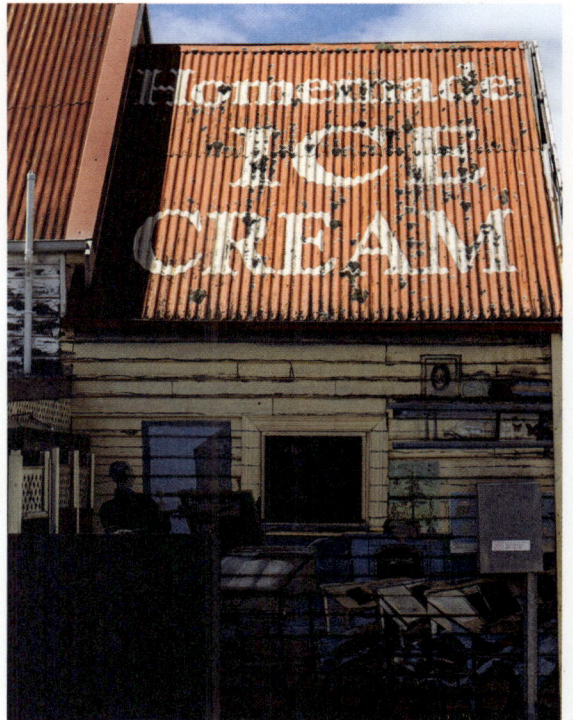

The shop did quite well until the global financial crisis in 2008 and tourists stopped coming. So the Zhaos decided to turn the shop into a Chinese restaurant, despite having no restaurant experience. 'Every Chinese family knows how to cook in a way. It's just trying to cater to the Australian palate,' says Alex. As research, the Zhaos went to Launceston to eat at a Chinese restaurant – just a few weeks before opening.

On opening night, there were many dockets of orders, but the food wasn't quite right. 'We thought we could figure it out, but my dad made a beef and black bean and it tasted nothing like it,' says Alex, who then googled a recipe for beef and black bean. 'The family knew nothing about farming and nothing about running a restaurant, but they kept going because it was about survival,' says Sammi. 'Both Alex and his dad are perfectionists, so that drive to get things perfect really pushed them.'

One night a customer complained that their lamb wasn't good. Alex suggested to his parents that they use their own lamb from the farm. The restaurant began serving paddock to plate long before they told customers that's what they were doing. When the Dorper sheep that Alex raised started to win awards, ABC Rural did a radio story on him, where he told listeners about T's. 'I said that if they wanted to try the lamb, they should come to our restaurant.' The farming community got behind Alex and T's, and things turned around. 'I feel a real sense of pride growing my own organic product and then putting it into the restaurant,' says Alex. 'How many people get to do that?'

Business is good these days, and Alex and Sammi have never been so busy, with a restaurant and a farm to run, and a family of seven children to care for. It's not a lifestyle that they want for their kids, though. 'No, they're going to be lawyers,' laughs Alex. 'We won't stop them taking on the restaurant, but we won't encourage it,' says Sammi. 'It suits our lifestyle, but it's full on. It's a lot of work. I hope they go and enjoy the world.'

PAN-FRIED POTSTICKERS

The potstickers at T's show off their free-range Berkshire pork and are served with a crispy golden lattice that's almost too beautiful to break into with your chopsticks. These Northern Chinese-style dumplings can easily be frozen and be cooked from frozen – just add six minutes to the cooking time. To save time, you can use store-bought dumpling wrappers, but these do not have the pleasing chewiness of homemade wrappers.

MAKES AROUND 36 (COOK IN BATCHES OF 12)

1½ tablespoons vegetable or canola oil
½ cup water
hot chilli oil, to serve

DOUGH

250 g plain flour
150 ml water
1 teaspoon vegetable oil
plain flour, extra, for dusting and rolling

FILLING

250 g pork mince
125 g Chinese cabbage (wombok), finely chopped
125 g garlic chives, finely chopped
½ onion, finely chopped
½ teaspoon five spice powder
1 tablespoon hoisin sauce
1 tablespoon oyster sauce
1 teaspoon salt
100 ml water
1 teaspoon sesame oil

LATTICE (FOR EVERY 12 POTSTICKERS)

1½ teaspoons self-raising flour
50 ml water

To make the dough, place the plain flour in a large bowl and pour in the water gradually while shaping a loose dough with your hands. Depending on the temperature and humidity of the room, you may need more or less water.

Transfer to a floured benchtop and knead the dough until smooth. Transfer the dough back to the bowl, cover and rest for 1 hour

Meanwhile, make the filling. Combine all the filling ingredients in a bowl. Mix well in a circular motion in only one direction to bind the protein and keep in the moisture.

Once the dough has rested, divide the dough into 3 sections. Roll each section into a rope around 2 cm in diameter, then cut each section into 12 equal pieces. Dust the pieces with extra flour to prevent them from sticking. Press each piece with the palm of the hand into a small disc.

Using a rolling pin, roll the discs out into thin circular wrappers. Place 1 tablespoon of the filling in the middle of each wrapper, fold over one side of the wrapper to cover the filling, and either pleat or pinch the edges together. You can moisten the edges of the wrapper with a wet fingertip before folding to help seal the wrapper.

Place the wrapped dumplings on a tray lined with baking paper or plastic wrap to prevent them from sticking. You can either cook these dumplings straight away or freeze them.

Heat vegetable or canola oil in a medium non-stick frying pan over medium–high heat. Arrange 12 dumplings in the pan, with space around them. Pour in ½ cup of water and immediately cover the pan with a lid. Turn down the heat to low–medium.

To make the lattice, mix the self-raising flour with the water until there are no lumps.

When the water has evaporated from the pan, around 8–10 minutes, lift the lid and pour in the lattice mixture. Cook, uncovered, for a further 2–3 minutes, or until lattice is golden and crispy.

Serve the dumplings on a plate, lattice side up, with hot chilli oil.

XINJIANG HAND-PULLED NOODLES WITH LAMB

For 4000 years, people have been making and eating hand-pulled noodles in north-western China, just east of Xinjiang. It became a staple during the Han Dynasty (206BC–AD220), and these days Xinjiang hand-pulled noodles (lahgman) are also popular in Kazakhstan, Kyrgyzstan and Russia. Alex says that the trick to making good hand-pulled noodles is to use high-protein flour, as the gluten content makes the noodles super chewy. Choose a good quality bread flour and you can't go wrong.

HAND-PULLED NOODLES

250 g bread flour

125 ml water

2 tablespoons olive oil or vegetable oil

SAUCE

120 g lamb fillet, sliced

½ teaspoon bicarbonate of soda

1 teaspoon cornflour

1 teaspoon shaoxing rice wine

1 teaspoon light soy sauce

3 tablespoon vegetable oil

½ onion, sliced

½ capsicum, sliced

1 baby bok choy, chopped

2 tablespoons broad bean chilli paste (doubanjiang) – Alex recommends Pixian brand

1 tablespoon dark soy sauce

To make the hand-pulled noodles, mix flour and water in a bowl to form a dough. Transfer to a floured benchtop, knead until smooth and then return to bowl. Cover and leave to rest for 20 minutes.

Cut the dough into 2 sections. Cover with the oil and roll each section into a long rope around 1.5cm in diameter.

In a large flat-bottomed dish, coil sections together into a spiral. Cover and rest for 1 hour.

Bring a large pot of water to the boil.

Hold the coil lightly with one hand, and whilst pinching the end with your other hand, stretch the coil into a very thick noodle. Loop the thick noodle around the first 3 fingers of both hands as if you are playing cat's cradle. Stretch the noodle out in a bouncing motion and smack the middle of the noodle cords onto the benchtop, around 5 times to get desired thickness.

Drop the noodles in the pot and cook for 2–3 minutes. Drain and set aside.

To make the sauce, combine the lamb, bicarb, cornflour, shaoxing wine and light soy sauce in a bowl. Set aside for 20 minutes.

Heat 2 tablespoons of the vegetable oil on high heat and add the lamb mixture. Stir-fry for 2 minutes or until cooked. Drain on a plate lined with paper towel.

Heat the remaining vegetable oil in the wok, add onion, capsicum, bok choy, broad bean chilli paste and dark soy sauce. Stir-fry for 1 minute and then add the noodles and lamb. Toss vigorously to break up the noodles and coat them in the sauce.

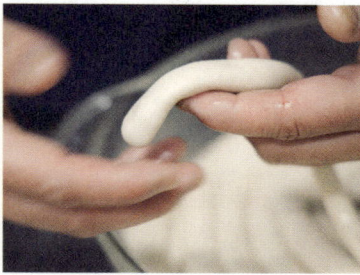

BEEF WITH BLACK BEAN

This is an essential Chinese restaurant dish, but what makes T's version stand out is they use their grass-fed, highly marbled Angus beef straight from their farm. Although you might not have access to such fresh produce, Sammi suggests using a lean beef to make the recipe, like a rump cut. We've included T's homemade black bean sauce recipe below, which will make you a larger-than-store-bought jar of sauce. You can also use store-bought black bean sauce.

½ zucchini, halved lengthways and sliced

4 broccoli florets

1 bok choy, roughly chopped

3 tablespoons vegetable oil

150 g beef, sliced

½ red capsicum, sliced

½ onion, sliced

2 tablespoons water

BLACK BEAN SAUCE

300 g whole fermented black beans

½ onion

½ cup light soy sauce

¾ cup dark soy sauce

3 garlic cloves

2 tablespoons sugar

1 teaspoon chilli powder

To make the black bean sauce, blitz half the black beans with all the other ingredients in a food processor until it forms a smooth paste. Transfer to an airtight container and stir in the remaining whole black beans. Keep refrigerated and use within 3 months.

Bring a pot of water to the boil, add the zucchini, broccoli and bok choy and cook for around 2 minutes. Drain and set aside.

Heat 2 tablespoons of oil in a wok on high heat, add the beef and stir-fry until almost cooked, around 2 minutes. Don't overcook the beef in this step. Drain on a plate lined with paper towel.

Heat the remaining oil in the wok on high heat, add the capsicum and onion and stir to coat. Add 1½ tablespoons black bean sauce, and then the water, green vegetables and beef. Toss well for 1 minute. Remove from heat and serve.

MEMORIES FROM AROUND AUSTRALIA

1990s–2010s

The Capitol Restaurant in Townsville, Queensland, has served my family members' meals for six generations: my great grandmother (who was three-quarters Chinese), through to my children and some of my cousins' grandchildren. The ham and chicken roll is our family fave, and we get takeaway for any of our family members who are not with us. We put it in the car fridge and take it home 1000 kilometres to Mount Isa for them.

JOANNE REAL

After watching the 2016 AFL grand final in a local pub, in which the Western Bulldogs broke their sixty-two-year drought, my wife and I went to our local Chinese restaurant, Lion Dance Chinese Restaurant in Williamstown, Victoria, to celebrate with some friends. The atmosphere in Lion Dance was electric – the restaurant, and most of the diners, were decked out in red, white and blue. Frank, the owner and a one-eyed Doggies supporter, was in particularly fine form. He had been at the match and came back to the restaurant to celebrate with everyone. He ended up being enthusiastically crowd-surfed through the dining room, as we tucked into our Singapore chicken and Mongolian beef. One of my favourite memories of a favourite restaurant.

PHIL PEERS

My parents owned Prince Court Chinese Restaurant in Yeronga, Brisbane, from 1990 to 2004. There are a mix of emotions from my memories as a restaurant kid. There's the delight of having a whole restaurant as your playground, endless access to soft drink, dessert and whatever Chinese dish off the menu on demand, and the joy of making new friends every night. But then there was also the pain of watching my parents slave away day and night, the strange feeling of resentment over their absence at my school recitals, and the fear of being vulnerable to being robbed at night, especially when we closed shop and were the only people around in our block. That's why we moved to Brisbane, because of the crime in Sydney. My parents were held up one night in their restaurant in Yagoona in Sydney while us kids slept comfortably upstairs. Now as a thirty-seven-year-old woman, I feel nothing but gratitude for my parents' hard work, and wish I had been a little more helpful and understanding as a child.

LUCY LIM

I grew up as a Chinese restaurant kid at Branxton Chinese Takeaway in Branxton, New South Wales, which opened in 1993. Of course there were going to be a few racist comments here and there, as we lived in a community that is predominantly white and I was one of less than ten Asians at my high school. Luckily, I had a close friend whose parents also owned a Chinese restaurant (Yee's Chinese Cuisine) less than 200 metres from my parents' one, so we shared a lot of experiences and we had each other to lean on during those years. Unfortunately, we would also get mistaken for the other frequently at school.

I also remember being upset at times for not being able to attend friends' birthday parties that were scheduled on the weekend at night because my parents would tell me I would need to help them work as it could get quite busy. Seeing the photos after each party on social media and hearing about it at school would make me feel so jealous as I would come home from work smelling like onions and fried rice with maybe an oil burn while my friends were having fun. The stress of balancing studying for the HSC and helping my parents work was a tough period for me.

However, throughout my childhood working at the shop, there have been many loyal customers that came in for takeaway. Since moving out of home to attend university and work in Sydney, I've been visiting home during the holiday periods. When I happen to also be working with my parents, it is a delight to catch up with customers and reminisce on the days that were. Some even recall when I was still an infant bouncing around the waiting area with some toys.

Even now, I'm turning thirty years old this year and still will help my parents work at the shop when I come back home to visit during the holidays.

SHELLY YAM

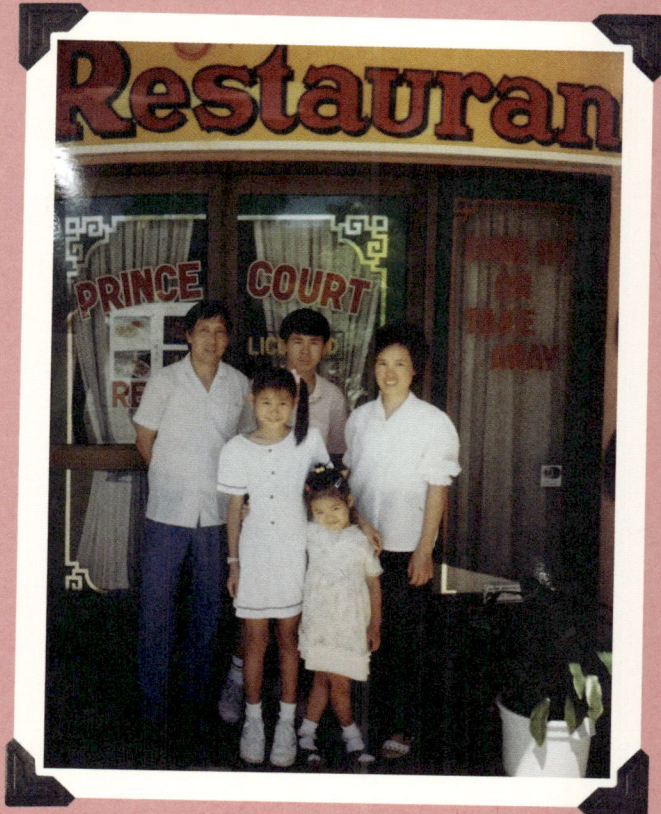

We spent most of our lives around Chinese restaurants. Our dad worked in them, knowing many in the industry, and a number of my parents' friends - immigrants or refugees - owned or worked in restaurants, although most have retired now.

Most people only see the hustle and boisterous cacophony that is your local Chinese restaurant. They don't see the many, many hours of work that are undertaken every day to run them. I've seen the exhaustion of our family friends as they've given absolutely everything to run these restaurants, and my dad as he worked the long service hours - coming home for a quick nap during the closing time between the lunch and dinner service. Chinese restaurants will always have a special place in my heart as they represent the grit and determination of those working to create a better life for their families and themselves.

BRENDA DILIZIA

THANK YOU

To the ten families we visited around Australia, for taking time out of your busy lives to share your personal stories and much-loved recipes. We appreciate you so much, and are grateful for the opportunity to share your stories.

To everyone at the ABC who made the show possible: The executive team who greenlit our idea, David Hua, Scott Spark, Kath Earle, Michelle Frampton and Jo Chichester. Our production team, Rachel Robinson, Carly Mooney and Linda Yilmaz. Our intrepid crew, Susan Lumsdon and Adam Toole, who always had enough room for an extra honey prawn and deep-fried ice cream. Our editor, Kenny Ang, who beautifully wove the stories together for screen. And to all the ABC production staff who contributed to *Chopsticks or Fork?*

To the Hardie Grant team, especially Emily Hart, who first had the idea for the book. Thank you also to Ruby Goss, Pam Brewster, Ana Jacobsen, Celia Mance, Rochelle Fernandez, Alex McDivitt, and your colleagues for your dedication to these stories.

To our agent, Benython Oldfield, for your smarts, unwavering support, and excellent humour.

To the Australian Embassy in Beijing, who inspired The Lost Cousins of Australian Chinese Dishes. To our experts: historians Sophie Couchman and Gordon Grimwade, and cultural consultant Lydia Feng.

To Annette Shun Wah and Greg Aitken, authors of *Banquet: Ten Courses to Harmony,* for paving the way when it comes to telling stories about Chinese restaurants in Australia.

To Larissa Dubecki, whose Qantas Travel Insider magazine article introduced us to several of the restaurants we visited.

Lin Jie: Thanks to my husband Sebastien, who was there at the germination of *Chopsticks or Fork?* in Karuah, and continually held down the fort at home whilst I trapesed around Australia to eat Chinese food, make a TV show, and then a book. Your endless support and patience kept me sane as we sauntered through the trials and tribulations of such a project.

To my parents and my brother Kevin. Thanks always for the extra food, for I know that is nothing but pure love. To my sweet little Gaspard, thanks for enjoying the hospitality of our restaurant families in utero and letting Mummy do her work.

And lastly, to Jen. Who knew when we met all those years ago in the ABC foyer, what a creative powerhouse WongKong would become? Thanks for being the best of friends, my creative confidante, and somebody I hope to send memes to 'til we are super old and super grey.

Jennifer: To Mum and Dad. You worked so hard for us. Thank you for your love, care, and companionship. I could only tell these stories because of what you taught me.

To AJ, my pun-believable brother. Thank you for your encouragement and for believing in me.

To my aunts and uncles for always looking after me, and for sharing your love of food and Chinese culture with enthusiasm.

To my cousins, my earliest dining companions, and my present-day food influencers.

To Claudia Au and Jason To. Thank you for your friendship, encouragement, and world-class organisation and management of *Chopsticks or Fork?*-related events.

To my friends and mentors (friendtors!), Annette Shun Wah, Jane Hutcheon, Electra Manikakis, and Katherine Tamiko Arguile for your care, guidance, and willingness to meet and eat.

For your friendship, thank you to Anna Lin and Lap Leung, David Hua and Ben May, Luke Tribe and Mikey Hankin, Scott Spark and Benjamin Law, CJ Delling and Alanis, and the Thursday Super Chilled Out POC "Writing Group".

To Lin Jie, for following your appetite to a Chinese restaurant in Karuah. I'm so grateful that your cravings led to us travelling together to every Australian state and territory for such meaningful and delicious reasons. What wonderful fortune to get to eat, laugh (and cry), and work with one of my best friends, even though you made me paddle a dragon boat in Hervey Bay. Thank you, pengyou.*
*friend in Chinese

IMAGE CREDITS

The following have been reproduced with permission from their copyright holders. Listed by page number.

9: Australian Broadcasting Corporation

11: (bottom) Australian Broadcasting Corporation

17 (bottom right), 19 (top right): Ernest and Whitney Lai

37 (bottom left): Leon, May Har and Melika Toy

70–71: Graeme Lindsay

72–73: Julia Mills

74–75: Janice Leong

76: Deidre Aftanas

77: Ruby Lee

81 (bottom left), 82 (bottom right): Gavin Chan

101: Emily Ng

119, 120 (top left and top right): Jason and Daniel Lee

134–135: Kelly Parsons

136: Derren Lowe

137: Lisa Adderly

138: Luke Tribe

139: Lily Ma

140–141: Catherine Wu

142–143: Steffie Yee

144–145: King Yin Lui

185: Vinh Chiem

198–199: Joshua Burns

216–219: Lucy Lim

221: Australian Broadcasting Corporation

Memories from Around Australia elements © Shutterstock (adhesive tape: Tortoon; black photo corners: Carolyn Franks)

Published in 2024 by Hardie Grant Books, an imprint of Hardie Grant Publishing

Hardie Grant Books (Melbourne)
Wurundjeri Country
Building 1, 658 Church Street
Richmond, Victoria 3121

Hardie Grant Books (North America)
2912 Telegraph Ave
Berkeley, California 94705

hardiegrant.com/books

Hardie Grant acknowledges the Traditional Owners of the Country on which we work, the Wurundjeri People of the Kulin Nation and the Gadigal People of the Eora Nation, and recognises their continuing connection to the land, waters and culture. We pay our respects to their Elders past and present.

A catalogue record for this book is available from the National Library of Australia

Chopsticks or Fork?
ISBN 978 1 74379 939 0
ISBN 978 1 74358 939 7 (ebook)

10 9 8 7 6 5 4 3 2 1

Publisher: Emily Hart, Pam Brewster
Head of Editorial: Jasmin Chua
Project Editor: Ruby Goss, Ana Jacobsen
Editor: Rochelle Fernandez
Design Manager: Kristin Thomas
Designer: Celia Mance
Head of Production: Todd Rechner
Production Controller: Jessica Harvie

Colour reproduction by Splitting Image Colour Studio
Printed in China by Leo Paper Products LTD.

MIX
Paper | Supporting responsible forestry
FSC® C020056

The paper this book is printed on is from FSC®-certified forests and other sources. FSC® promotes environmentally responsible, socially beneficial and economically viable management of the world's forests.